PRODUCTIVITY:
THE
★AMERICAN
ADVANTAGE

How 50 U.S. companies are regaining the competitive edge

L. William Seidman
and
Steven L. Skancke

A TOUCHSTONE BOOK
Published by Simon & Schuster
NEW YORK   LONDON   TORONTO   SYDNEY   TOKYO   SINGAPORE

Touchstone
Simon & Schuster Building
Rockefeller Center
1230 Avenue of the Americas
New York, New York 10020

Copyright © 1989, 1990 by L. William Seidman and Steven L. Skancke

First Touchstone Edition 1991
Designed by Levavi & Levavi
Manufactured in the United States of America

1   3   5   7   9   10   8   6   4   2   Pbk.

Library of Congress Cataloging in Publication Data
Seidman, Lewis William, date.
Productivity, the American advantage: how 50 U.S. companies
are regaining the competitive edge/L. William Seidman and
Steven L. Skancke.—1st Touchstone ed.
p.   cm.
Rev. ed. of: Competitiveness—the executive's guide to success.
© 1989.
"A Touchstone book."
Includes index.
1. Industrial productivity—United States—Case studies.
I. Skancke, Steven L.   II. Seidman. Lewis William, date.
Competitiveness—the executive's guide to success.   III. Title.
HC110.I52S45   1991
338.7'0973—dc20   90-28745
CIP
ISBN 0-671-70219-X
ISBN 0-671-74030-X Pbk.

This is a revised edition of a work originally published under the title
Competitiveness: The Executive's Guide To Success.

CONTENTS

Know where you are going and how you plan to get there, and be flexible and persistent in the pursuit of defined goals 17 • First things first, every day 18 • Measure everyone's productivity—including your own 18 • Be a mobile communicator 18 • Coordinate and control 19 • Computers are the key to productivity improvement 19 • Seek out and remove obstacles to productivity 19 • Reward your producers 20 • Encourage innovation, even if you have to ruffle a few feathers 20 • Expect and accept only quality 20 • Be enthusiastic 21 • Act now! 21 • Stay healthy, be happy 21

Start productivity programs at the top 22 • Reduce layers of management 23 • Spread accountability throughout

Certified Grocers of California Ltd. • Champion International • Como Plastics • ComSonics Incorporated • Continental Insurance Company • Dana Corporation • Diamond Fiber Products (formerly Diamond International) • Donnelly Corporation • Farmers Home Administration (FmHA) • Ford Motor Company • GE's Daytona Simulation and Control Systems • GE's Meter and Control Business Department • GE's Erie Locomotive Plant • Great Salt Lake Minerals and Chemicals Corporation • Hewitt Associates • Hewlett-Packard Company • Honeywell Inc. • Hughes Aircraft Company • Humana Inc. • Huron Machine Products, Inc. • Intel Corporation • Joint Labor Management Committee, Retail Food Industry • Kitchell Corporation • Lincoln Electric Company • Lowe's Companies, Inc. • McCreary Tire & Rubber Company • Motorola, Inc. • New United Motor Manufacturing Inc. • New York City Department of Sanitation • Nucor Corporation • Palatine Police Department • PENNTAP • Prince Corporation • The Procter & Gamble Company • Productivity and Responsibility Increase Development and Employment (PRIDE) • The Prudential Insurance Company of America • Shippers' Associations • Softool Corporation • The Travelers Insurance Company • TRW Inc. • UAW-Ford National Education Development and Training Program • Westinghouse Electric Corporation

INTRODUCTION

A competitor is the guy who goes in a revolving door behind you and comes out ahead of you.

That's how George Romney, the former cabinet member, governor of Michigan, and CEO of American Motors, defines a competitor. Such a feat might seem impossible, but that is exactly what happened to scores of American companies in the decades of the 1970s and 1980s. They went into the revolving door of the world marketplace first only to discover that foreign competitors were somehow coming out ahead of them. Any number of explanations have been offered for that surprising and unprecedented turn of events, but far more important in the decade of the 1990s is finding the answer to one crucial question: How can American companies regain their ability to compete in the world marketplace to make sure that we again come out ahead?

Productivity has become the major issue facing businesses, governments, and institutions concerned with rebuilding America's ability to compete. It is an issue that we have studied for nearly a decade, beginning in 1982 and 1983 as directors of the White House Conference on Productivity, when we examined the competitive strategies of nearly a thousand companies and organizations, large and small, sharpening our focus to several hundred of them in 1984. Then in 1987, and again in 1989, we reexamined many of these organizations to determine how well their strategies had fared over time. Our study has convinced us that competitiveness is not simply a function of national policies, but of thousands of competitive individual companies working to improve their productivity and their positions in the world marketplace. Ultimately, the fate of America's competitiveness depends upon individual company initiatives.

Our studies of successful people, ideas, operations, and strategies have also led us to the conclusion that while much that is new is being used, most of what succeeds is based on traditional American attitudes and values set in our modern environment. In fact, America has always had the competitive advantage. By applying the principles that made us great in the first place, we can rebuild the base needed to increase our productivity, improve our ability to compete, and resolve our national economic problems as well. To secure our place in world competition, our best resources must be used, our best ideas must be implemented, and our best people must be put to the task. Above all, we must use the fundamental strengths that built our past success.

"American Exceptionalism"

The American advantage in a world economic competition can be found in the special strengths of our multicultural, democratic, capitalistic roots. The great observer of America, Alexis de Tocqueville, described it as "American exceptionalism." Americans are exceptional because of our independence, individuality, and desire for freedom. We have a pioneer tradition of wanting to make it on our own. We are innovators, entrepreneurs, rugged individualists. These traditional American attitudes are just what is needed to meet world competition. Americans will succeed by returning to their roots.

Even beyond these traditional values, the American advantage also derives from the unparalleled abundance of our natural and human resources. Our standard of living is among the highest in the world; our work force is highly skilled and strongly motivated. We have the most advanced technology and a solid industrial infrastructure. We have access to capital and the world's largest consumer market. We share a common language and a common work ethic. Even with their imperfections, our democratic government and free-enterprise system are major American advantages. We have only to utilize our many social, economic, and political strengths to win in the global competition that lies ahead.

World-Class Competitors

Many American companies are already in the vanguard of world-class competition. They are not there by accident. They have leaders who plan and organize for their success, who know where the company is heading, and who communicate their strategy all the way down the line. They make sure their organization is flexible and that decisions can be made quickly in the midst of battle. The emphasis in these companies is always on quality and better management of all resources in order to improve their productivity and their ability to compete. And last, but by no means least, they recognize that their employees are the key to their growth and success.

The old saying that there is nothing new under the sun applies to many of the competitive strategies we have observed in action in these companies. But rediscovery can be just as useful as finding out about ideas for the first time. And some of these strategies belie the old saying by being truly innovative.

Among the many companies we studied that have combined both the old and the new to regain their competitive edge are the following.

Diamond Fiber Products. Implementing a comprehensive program for rewarding employees who do their job well, Diamond increased output 16.5 percent and accrued savings of $5 million in only eighteen months.

Como Plastics Corporation. By adopting a people-oriented approach to management that emphasizes teamwork, Como doubled sales and increased profits over 800 percent during a three-year period.

Donnelly Corporation. Applying a variety of reward systems over a seven-year period, including profit sharing and participative management, Donnelly reaped a 220 percent return on investment.

Certified Grocers. By adopting suggestions made by its employees—and by rewarding outstanding workers with paid time off—Certified increased its productivity by 15 percent in one year, while saving more than $2 million in payroll costs.

Champion International. Organized into problem-solving teams, Champion's employees solved stubborn productivity-related issues that saved the company $7 million in the paper division alone.

Lowe's Companies, Inc. By making employees owners through ESOPs (employee stock ownership plans), Lowe's transformed itself into one of America's fastest-growing corporations. Within three decades, it grew from three stores to more than two hundred, while boosting profits from $18 million to $900 million.

Palatine (Illinois) Police Department. Providing an alternative to traditional promotions through a dual-career ladder, the Palatine Police Department found a new way to motivate police personnel and increased productivity by 100 percent.

These companies and many others are using the American advantage to win the competitive battle. Our studies of the techniques and strategies they have put to use have convinced us that American companies still have what it takes to once again become world-class competitors. With all the advantages inherent in our way of life, the opportunity to meet the competition and to be number one is still available to any American company willing to take up the challenge.

This book highlights what a diverse group of American companies and public organizations is doing to improve their own productivity and competitiveness—and hence their profitability. In Part I we describe the broad techniques and strategies that we believe will offer you the best chance to improve the competitive position of your own company. These ideas are illustrated by examples from a wide spectrum of American companies supplemented by interviews with the people who have implemented these ideas and seen them work successfully. More specific cost-saving and profit-making strategies are detailed in the individual corporate case studies in Part II of the book. By adapting and implementing these strategies, we believe you can bring about exciting and dynamic changes in your own workplace. The recommendations are not faddish; they are deeply rooted in the American tradition of individuality, ingenuity, and hard work. And they will enable you, too, to come out of the revolving door ahead of the competition.

PART I

MAKING IT HAPPEN

CHAPTER 1

INNOVATIVE MANAGEMENT: Thirteen Guidelines for Coming Out on Top

To be a successful competitor, you have to be a successful manager, and a successful manager is a leader. But what is a leader? Though definitions and descriptions vary, almost all managers agree that a leader is someone who sets an example for others to follow. Rather than trying to identify leadership traits through "empirical" studies, we listened to successful managers talk about their own guidelines for leadership. From the hundreds of testimonies we gathered, certain themes emerged.

Know Where You Are Going and How You Plan to Get There, and Be Flexible and Persistent in the Pursuit of Defined Goals

Let workers know what your objectives are—both short term and long term. The old adage "If you don't know where you're going, any road will do" is just as true on the factory floor as it is in the boardroom. Nothing is more important than mobilizing everyone toward a common goal.

First Things First, Every Day

Decide each day what is most important in terms of meeting your objectives. Get organized and disciplined. Make a "to-do" list at the start of each day, then do the hardest, least pleasant tasks first.

Measure Everyone's Productivity—Including Your Own

Unless you are measuring your productivity, you will not know whether you are on course, off course, or ready to crash. Measures can and should be simple. The best are usually the ones developed by the individuals or groups being measured. In fact, many managers and employees already have informal measures that they subconsciously use to answer questions like "Why should I promote this employee instead of another?" and "Why do I deserve a raise or a promotion?"

But try not to get bogged down in the trappings of an intricate measurement system. No system is worth extraordinary hours or costs, so use data that already exist or can be easily assembled.

Be a Mobile Communicator

Walk around, talk, look, listen, and spread the word. When you are confined to your office, you do not have access to your most valuable asset: your people. Communication also means listening, so let your employees know that you want to hear from them, and then hear them out.

The key to communication is attitude. A "Be reasonable, do it my way" approach will not make the grade. Be willing to become a partner in a joint process, not a commander in the field. Partnership is not an abdication of authority, but rather a productivity tool. Time after time, managers usually find that it is the front-line worker who knows more about how to correct productivity problems than anyone else.

One very difficult thing for a manager to do is to drop the natural defense mechanism. Instead of giving the automatic response "We always do it this way," a manager should try to see the issue from the side of the person asking the question. Being mobile also means being able to move 180 degrees to the other side of the situation.

Coordinate and Control

Managers must coordinate procedures, processes, and people. They must be able to provide integration and leadership, and delegate responsibility. The manager's ability to coordinate and control the operation is, in the end, the reason that the product turns out to be the desired horse instead of the proverbial camel.

Control does not necessarily mean centralized decision-making, but it does mean a certain amount of supervision. And the manager's methods of supervision must constantly be revised, because each day brings new challenges as people and production methods change.

Computers Are the Key to Productivity Improvement

Computers are the most important new tool for enhancing productivity. Whether you are involved in manufacturing or a service industry or are self-employed, computers can provide information, control operations, and monitor quality at a relatively low cost.

Being technologically aware and up-to-date is a major challenge. As computers become more inexpensive, more powerful, and more "user friendly," they will become an even more important component of future productivity plans.

Seek Out and Remove Obstacles to Productivity

Let employees know that you are serious about eliminating productivity barriers by organizing a "search-and-destroy" mission. Ask all your people to list what they see as obstacles to their own productivity, then have them list the obstacles they see to the company's overall productivity and efficiency. When the obstacles are clearly identified, have the courage to remove them no matter whose territory is invaded.

Reward Your Producers

Employees are your greatest resource. Why not let them know it? Reward those who help you, and not just by fattening their paychecks. Peer recognition, for example, is a powerful motivator, so capitalize on it.

And remember, gainsharing has no net cost. Employee ownership contributes to a sense of a common future, because all owners have a vested interest in making their organization work.

Encourage Innovation, Even If You Have to Ruffle a Few Feathers

Entrepreneurs are created by working with entrepreneurs, because the acceptance of new ideas forces learning and change. The biggest paybacks come from ideas that change the product, the process, and the people.

Gains in productivity require innovation, change, flexibility, and adaptability. Every good system borrows from the past and attempts to innovate for the future, and each problem requires its own solution. "We always do it this way" is a sure formula for frozen productivity and loss of competitive position.

Expect and Accept Only Quality

To achieve quality, you must ask for it, expect it, require it, and reward it. Excellence breeds excellence. Without quality, you will not have any customers, and without customers, you will not have a business.

Be Enthusiastic

A happy environment is a productive environment, so play the company cheerleader and emphasize a can-do approach to work. Remember that enthusiasm is contagious, and so is defeatism. So learn to accept problems as opportunities, not as harbingers of doom and despair.

Act Now!

Fix it, move it, try it, explore it, and go for it. We seldom fail for lack of good ideas, but we will always fail if we do not act on them. So be opportunistic and take risks. Set deadlines, and if you miss them, set new ones. Above all, act!

Stay Healthy, Be Happy

Energetic management requires a healthy body and a sound mind. No job is worth endangering your health, so stay in good physical shape and leave your worries at the company doorstep. And encourage your employees to stay healthy too. As in golf—where you have to keep your left arm (or whichever is *your* leading arm) straight, head down, eye on the ball, shift your weight, and follow through—learning all these management guidelines may seem like a lot to handle in one lesson.

So feel free to integrate them into your management style one by one and embellish them with your own imagination and specialized knowledge.

CHAPTER 2

ORGANIZATION:
Strategies to Improve Your Competitive Edge

Becoming a winner does not happen by accident. If you want to win—to be productive, profitable, and competitive —then you have to organize yourself to make it happen. Although techniques for getting organized may vary widely, we have identified ten organizational maxims common to companies that have successfully become productive competitors.

Start Productivity Programs at the Top

Without the endorsement of senior management, no productivity plan can really succeed, no competition can be won. "You have to say it at the top and mean it all the way down," says Don Gross of Certified Grocers of California, a grocery wholesaler. The Dana Corporation, a vehicular-components manufacturer with thousands of employees, demonstrates its concern for productivity by making sure that every employee meets with a senior-level manager at least once a year. And the company chairman lets everyone know of his concerns, goals, and personal views through a quarterly letter to employees. At Prince Corporation, an auto-parts manufacturer, president John Spoelhof shows his support and concern by personally reviewing 70 to 80 percent of all quarterly personnel reports.

Reduce Layers of Management

Reducing management layers not only lowers overall costs, it also enhances communication. You've heard the saying: "With each layer of management, 50 percent of the message being passed down the line is lost." Today, the spokes of the wheel are replacing the pyramid as the structure most widely copied by productive organizations. This organizational structure allows for stronger participation, increased input, and greater consideration of a wide variety of viewpoints.

"One steel company has thirty-two levels of management between the first-line supervisor and the senior executive," says Carla O'Dell, a Houston-based management consultant. Compare that to Apple Computer: "We [had] three levels of management—and I was one of them," said Steven Jobs, the company's founder, who is now leading a new entrepreneurial enterprise.

Spread Accountability throughout the Organization

Pushing responsibility down the organizational ladder to the "hands-on" working level is a common ingredient of many successful productivity plans. "Never tell people how to do things. Tell them what to do and they will surprise you with their ingenuity," says one savvy manager. "Delegation goes all the way down the line to the key person—the most important manager of all—that is, the person who actually produces the product."

At American Seating, one of the largest producers of seating, responsibility for setting production goals rests with cost-reduction committees. These committees set their own goals for productivity improvement and determine a monetary value for the savings they hope to achieve. Once these goals are defined, the committee sets out to accomplish them as it sees fit, purchasing new machines or redesigning production lines if necessary.

At ComSonics, a Virginia cable TV products firm, all employees are stockholders; they are, therefore, considered one of the four levels of management and are expected to help in making important management decisions. For example, when the diagnostic and repair areas faced the problem of too little space, too little time, and too much work, a worker committee came up with a solution—adding a third shift with a 12 percent pay differential—even though it meant that some other workers would lose their overtime pay.

Make the Competitive Spirit an Integral Part of the Corporate Culture

Improving your competitiveness requires more than a new organizational chart: It requires a change in attitude. And this attitude must be reflected in your corporate culture. After all, corporate culture is what defines acceptable behavior, and a culture that integrates change, innovation, risk taking, cooperation, and quality is one that will lead to productivity improvement.

Successful managers are those who work to define and create the type of corporate culture that breeds productivity. "Create an organization where people share a sense of common fate—that is, a common productivity ethic," says one manager. "A corporate culture that develops a sharp pain in anyone who sees waste or inefficiency is the kind of attitude you want," explains another.

At Dana, the corporate culture constantly reflects the company's strong confidence in the individual. "We have a lot of folk sayings around here," notes a top official, "and one of them is that within your own twenty-five square feet, the person doing the job is the one who knows the most about it, and he's the expert. It's an attitude that's not easy to develop, but once you've got it, it's a marvelous tool."

Westinghouse decided to adopt a corporate culture that

emphasized cooperation. Time and motion study experts —traditionally hated figures in U.S. factories—began working with, not on, employees, and the results were immediate and obvious. "We began to see an unquantifiable but undeniably real improvement in the quality of work life around the division. Many people have indicated that they're more satisfied now with the scope and challenge of their jobs. We haven't undertaken a formal attitude survey, but the feedback is extremely positive. In the elevators and on the stairways, we hear remarks like 'I'm getting a lot more work done' and 'My job's more interesting now,' " says Charles C. Hoop, Westinghouse manager, now in their Marine Division and formerly in the Nuclear Technology Division.

Another good attitude to encourage concerns labor unions: Rather than working against them, adopt a corporate culture that fosters cooperation. At the Joint Labor Management Committee (JLMC) of the Retail Foods Industry, for instance, the corporate culture promotes a new awareness and sensitivity to labor problems. As a result, there is a less hostile atmosphere in collective bargaining.

Plan Ahead and Proceed Step by Step

Organizing for productivity requires action at all levels and in all parts of the business, but it cannot be done all at once. In fact, crash programs to increase productivity are not likely to succeed. Start small and build from there. Test your ideas with small groups before you implement them companywide, whether they concern people, technology, attitudes, or strategies. Successful programs are built piece by piece and evolve as required.

Diamond Fiber Products (formerly Diamond International) provides a good example of how to introduce change slowly. When Diamond conceived of the idea of the "100 Club" as a means of rewarding outstanding employees through recognition and gifts, it cautiously introduced the program at its egg-carton plant in Palmer, Massachusetts. The company's investment in both time and money was modest, but when an evaluation revealed impressive results—both in productivity (output increased 16.5 percent) and in attitude (grievances declined 43 percent)—Diamond introduced the club into four of its other plants. Success in these additional plants proved that this was an innovation worthy of expansion. As of today, personnel manager Dan Boyle has installed sixty similar programs in Diamond manufacturing and service organizations around the country.

Be Customer and Quality Oriented

Customers are what keeps any business in business, and today they demand quality and service. Keeping the customer satisfied is necessary for your continued existence.

Good quality requires the effective management of systems and processes. As one financial officer explains: "It's interesting to note that purely human mistakes are only a small minority of the errors that reduce quality in our business [Irving Trust Company]. In fact, less than 15 percent of the source of error derives from our account officers or operators, while 85 percent of the problems stem from the system—technological foul-ups or lack of communication. In other words, 85 percent of the errors require management action for prevention. Workers are really powerless in solving the bulk of the problems."

Productivity and quality are really two sides of the same coin. Productivity improves when there is an organized effort to equate quality with productivity, and poor quality can destroy any productivity program.

Keep the "Golden Rule" Golden

Respectful, considerate, and polite conduct between managers and workers is a common characteristic found in successful organizations. For Warren Braun, chief executive officer at ComSonics, consideration means treating everyone "as I would like to be treated." At Kollmorgen, a manufacturer of printed circuits, chairman Bob Swiggett notes: "We just assume that everybody's honest, and we run the business that way." Explains one Kollmorgen company official, "We preach trust and the Golden Rule, and we're very careful that what we do is the same as what we say. Once we had a book that said you get three days off if your mother or father dies, but if a neighbor dies that you've known for thirty-five years, you get no time off. We threw the book out."

Productivity gains are dependent upon the motivation of people and their enthusiasm for and commitment to corporate goals depend on the way they are treated. Consideration for others is the only way to create a winning team.

Find a Better Way—Look for New Ideas

"The way we always do it" may not be the best way to do it now. With new technologies and new methods of management being developed every day, the old way may very well be obsolete. It is important to examine every detail of your operation to determine if there is a better, more efficient way of doing things. Often there are better ways to manage the talents of others, reorganize, or simply change the way jobs are done.

Kollmorgen found that breaking units down into smaller sizes, for instance, helped transform its photocircuits operation. Prior to its merger with Kollmorgen, Photocircuits Corporation had been a pioneer in the manufacture of printed circuit boards. But one day, when Kollmorgen's chairman, Bob Swiggett, surveyed the production floor— five hundred workers, fifty process steps, fifteen departments, and one hundred open orders—he realized that the operations were in fact "a classic case of confusion. . . . [They] were lucky ever to ship anything."

In an attempt to solve this problem, Kollmorgen installed an elegant and expensive computerized control and production system. The computer worked beautifully, but the company's performance got worse. Foremen were preoccupied with printouts instead of people, and managers spent more time worrying about the internal systems than about customers.

Recognizing that the computer system had not eliminated the confusion, only computerized it, Swiggett went to the concept of small teams, which had worked out well in the old expediting department. Dividing the entire company into groups of about seventy-five people organized along product line or market segment, Swiggett made each team responsible for its own small profit center. "Almost magically," explains Swiggett, "everything improved. Customers were happier, pricing was better, profits rose, inventories turned faster, troublesome book-to-physical-inventory variance surprises disappeared. Morale rose with the evidence of success." After six months of the new decentralized system, output per employee had doubled and on-time deliveries improved from 60 percent to 90 percent.

Work simplification is another, often overlooked approach for gaining substantial benefits. When Como Plastics took a careful look at its assembly line, for example, it found that it could redesign the line to use one fewer employee and still achieve the same output. At Great Salt Lake Minerals and Chemicals Corporation, the minor change of rotating shifts forward instead of backward—in tune with workers' circadian rhythms—helped to keep shift employees awake and more productive.

Work simplification often requires no more than eliminating bureaucratic regulations that were developed long ago and then multiplied over the years and that may no longer be relevant. "Thirteen years ago," explains an official at Dana, "we had three volumes that defined our standard operating procedures. We threw them out. And there's an interesting story that goes along with that. It was our then president who decided that he'd really like to try a different way of running the company, so he went into the chairman with this armload of books and said, 'Say, I want to throw these out.' And the chairman said, 'Oh no, you can't do that, that's good stuff. You know it cost us a lot of money to develop it.' So the president said, 'Well, all

right, you tell me what the good stuff is and I'll keep that.'
The chairman replied, 'Well, I don't know, I've never read
the darn thing.' "

Invest! Invest! Invest!

Judicious investments must be made in equipment, computers, and new techniques and technologies. In today's
increasingly competitive business world, it is essential to
evaluate and plan for sound capital investments. Again and
again, successful companies have found that wise investments in technology pay for themselves many times over.

At Reynolds Aluminum, a $125 million overhaul in the
cold-running mill at its McCook aluminum steel and plate
plant in Brookfield, Illinois, increased employee output by
100 percent. The use of robots in GE's Daytona, Florida,
plant increased productivity by reducing errors and defects
42 percent.

For the Calvert Group, which manages financial funds,
investing in better telecommunications—long-distance 800
numbers, WATS lines, and a sophisticated phone system
that monitors the length of calls and number of calls on
hold—allowed the company to give its customers more efficient service. Now, employees know when to speed up
their phone conversations, because they always know just
how many customers are waiting to be served.

Train for the Competition

Training on a continuing basis is the hallmark of a good
competitor with a sound productivity program. The auto
industry, for example, has become a leader in implementing innovative training programs. At General Motor's
Orion, Michigan, plant workers and supervisors partici-
pated in an intensive three-week training course on teamwork and quality control that was designed to facilitate
employee acceptance of a plantwide technological upgrade. With an emphasis on changing attitudes toward
technology and on teaching new skills, workers were

trained in multi-task assembly operations. When the training was completed, a fully qualified worker could perform all the jobs in one part of the assembly line, enabling that person to fill in for other workers when the need arose.

A competitor, Ford Motor Company, is equally committed to training. It has teamed up with the United Auto Workers to form the Ford Employee Development and Training Program. The fifteen-plus courses it provides are designed to increase employee skills, productivity, and quality of life, and to retrain furloughed employees for new jobs.

Training is essential for managers as well as for labor. Champion International, a large conglomerate, identifies managers with high potential and places them in its "Managing for Excellence" program. At Hughes Aircraft, managers are trained not only to develop an understanding of productivity, but also to foster a dedicated commitment to productivity improvement in both themselves and those they supervise.

CHAPTER 3

PLANNING:
Strategies for Staying Ahead

Harland Cleveland* has defined strategic planning as the act of "innovating around a general sense of direction." The words "general sense of direction" are a key component of this definition, because no one has yet devised a way to plan in detail very far into the future. The future, perhaps fortunately, will always remain a mystery.

Set a Direction

The primary objective in setting a direction is to move ahead of the crowd or, as it is usually put, "get ahead of the curve." This concept is at the heart of the planning process and is the foundation for short-term, detailed planning that is necessary for improving productivity and competitive position.

It is top management's responsibility to determine what road to take—to define the "general direction." In order to do that, management needs to listen to employees and customers to make sure it is not heading down a dead-end

---

* Formerly president of the University of Hawaii; currently director of the Hubert H. Humphrey Institute at the University of Minnesota in St. Paul.

street. Once the general direction is determined, managers must then work to develop flexible strategies that can anticipate and respond to the inevitable changes in the marketplace.

If defining a general sense of direction is all there is to strategic planning, then why is so much attention paid to it? Because defining where to take the organization is the most important decision management must make.

Often companies within the same industry will make vastly different strategic-planning decisions. In the steel industry, for example, many companies have had to choose whether to remain solely in the steel business or to diversify. Bethlehem Steel has decided to devote itself almost exclusively to the manufacturing and processing of steel, whereas U.S. Steel has decided to expand in other directions. Having set their basic courses, however, both companies now must make future decisions based on their initial choice. The "general direction" is the signpost that affects each and every turn.

Once a company has defined its strategic plan, it can then explore proposals and actions designed to move the enterprise in that direction. No numbers are needed in this exercise, only ideas. The company must attempt to determine where its customers, its industry, and the general economy are headed, then move to take advantage of the changing environment.

Know Your Customer

How is this seemingly overwhelming feat achieved? Primarily through knowledge of and satisfaction of customer needs. That is why you have to study your customer thoroughly and ask yourself: What can be done to make my customer a happier person? Only by anticipating trends and directions, or even by creating new trends, can you get the jump on the competition. Frederick Webster, Jr., at Dartmouth's Tuck School of Business, puts it this way: "The most basic commitment of all must be to the customer: commitment to quality products and services, and innovative, timely solutions to customer problems." Knowing how to satisfy the customer can be the result of field work, marketing studies, personal observation, good guesswork, or even intuition. But no matter where it comes from, your knowledge of your customer is the key to improving your competitive position through planning.

Stay Flexible

No plan to satisfy the customer will work forever. Your customers operate in a dynamic environment, and their needs and desires change quickly. And since no one can accurately forecast the future, all strategic plans will involve some degree of risk.

An essential ingredient of good planning, therefore, is flexibility. Nothing is more destructive to a company's success than turning the strategy of today into an inviolate rule for tomorrow. The ultimate test of the quality of your planning is your ability to perceive that the weather has changed and you need to set a new course.

And often strategies must be altered quickly in spite of substantial resistance. Decisions to veer toward one direction rather than another, or even to make a U-turn, may cause conflicts among sales, product development, and manufacturing departments. For instance, it is not uncommon to hear the production chiefs complaining: "We just got this line running right, and now the guys in sales want to change it—and in forty-eight hours."

The need for quick change often results from a surprise market development or the introduction of a new product by a competitor. But even though changing quickly can be expensive, not changing quickly enough can be even more expensive. As an ancient Chinese proverb says, "If we can't change direction, we shall end up where we are headed."

Flexibility, then, becomes the watchword of those who must design, manufacture, or distribute a product, and a system of "planning for change" is essential. Technology can make "instant" change possible, because flexible manufacturing systems can reduce setup times for production

lines from weeks to minutes. But managers themselves
have to embrace the concept of flexibility first before new
technology can provide any advantage in the marketplace.

Tune In to Change

Many companies credit their success to the ability to combine an understanding of the customer's changing needs
with organizational flexibility. Federal Express, for instance, sized up the information explosion and perceived a
real need to move information faster from place to place.
The result was overnight package delivery—the first in the
country. Other companies now provide the same service,
but by getting there first, Federal Express set the pace in
the competition and has continued to run well ahead of
the pack.

Both Carl Eller, chairman of Circle K convenience
stores, and Robert Anderson, chairman of ARCO, examined customer needs and perceived a new trend in convenience shopping. They saw that consumers wanted two
commodities—gasoline and groceries—at one location. So
Circle K redesigned its convenience stores to include gas
pumps, while ARCO added convenience stores to its filling
stations.

The communications industry has also produced its
share of visionaries who beat the competition by anticipating customer needs. Since the beginning of radio, for example, many people had been losing money or going broke
attempting to put new FM stations on the air. Even though
FM broadcasting offered clear stereo reception, AM radio
had become the industry standard. In fact, most of the
public did not have FM receivers.

This situation, however, changed in the mid-1960s. Vi-
sionary broadcasters noticed a change under way when
Japanese manufacturers began selling AM/FM radio receivers as a strategy to penetrate the U.S. market. At the
time, there were no takers for over four hundred FM licenses available from the Federal Communications Commission (FCC), even in fast-growing markets of the

country—Aspen, Colorado, and Orlando, Florida. But then the beat-the-crowd strategists made their move into FM radio, and the same FM licenses that went begging in 1970 are worth hundreds of millions of dollars today.

Television provides another vivid example. In the fifties and sixties, the major networks dominated the television market, attracting both mass audiences and advertiser dollars, while independent and UHF stations were, for the most part, unprofitable. Broadcasters saw little reason to invest in these alternatives, which were generally perceived to be losers. Because of low demand, these licenses could be acquired from the FCC inexpensively and without costly and time-consuming competitive applications.

By 1976, the situation in the TV industry had changed. By providing an array of new channels, cable television had altered viewing patterns and many TV watchers were beginning to prefer counterprogramming. With network domination broken, independent stations that offered something different suddenly attracted sizable audiences and became very profitable. In Phoenix, Arizona, for example, anyone ahead of the crowd could have obtained the license for Channel 15 for practically nothing in the early 1970s, but about ten years later this "free" license had a value of more than $30 million.

This scenario was repeated across the country. In 1976, UHF licenses in small markets like Albany, San Antonio, and Omaha were awarded without competition. But by 1978, the few licenses that were still available in these cities were heavily contested—with between eight and ten bidders competing for each application. Being just a year or two ahead of the curve made the profitable difference.

Use the Home-Court Advantage

In the end, your company's resources are best spent when you know best where to spend them. So, find your niche. Profits are greatest when you alone have the right product, are producing it with the best combination of people, capital, and materials, and know how to sell it to anyone for whom it has real value. Successful planning focuses on finding your niche and making it profitable, while higher productivity is one of the objectives of planning. The ultimate goal is a successfully competitive and profitable enterprise.

CHAPTER 4

QUALITY:
Set Standards for Success

Nothing pleases a customer more than a *quality* product at a reasonable price. Yet many American companies today emphasize volume at the expense of quality. As a result, these companies, once considered the best in the world, have developed a reputation for mediocrity. Their quality standards have slipped from "high" to merely "acceptable," if that. These companies don't understand that quality is free. The fact is that money spent on quality control results in lower costs and overall savings.

If suppliers provide quality materials and workers prepare quality products, then sales forces can market more with less effort. If quality is a top priority, then every step of the production process requires less effort and results in more goods at lower cost. Sales and profits come naturally when quality and productivity work together.

Bruce Hill, a vice-president of Olin Corporation, a brass-fabricating company, explains his approach to quality this way: "Quality is everything that goes with having a satisfied and, hopefully, a continuing customer. It's not just product quality; it's the quality of service, of responsiveness, and of error-free delivery."

Quality Starts at the Top

"Unless you receive the support of the CEO and president," one executive told us, "you're not going to get to first base. Your commitment to quality should be reflected throughout your company, from the purchasing specifications given to parts and material suppliers all the way through to the delivery of the final product."

Olin Corporation has firsthand experience with how a commitment to quality at the top pays off in productivity. When the company discovered that its customers viewed Olin products as merely "satisfactory," it decided to make quality a top priority. Senior managers went down the line to every worker and explained how things were going to change. They emphasized that inferior products were no longer acceptable, and that Olin could only survive by making a commitment to produce only the best.

Once the message was heard, things began to happen quickly. Special task forces were assembled to find new ways to improve product quality. Workers at all levels became involved in identifying and correcting problems. The company trained employees to manage quality-assurance programs and practice statistical quality control.

As a result of this commitment, the quality of Olin's products began to improve significantly. Customers clearly were more satisfied. Within five years, product rejections dropped by 83 percent. In one product line that accounted for $14 million in sales, Olin received only $154 worth of returned merchandise. At the same time, the quality of work life improved for all Olin employees and union grievances against the company dropped dramatically.

Get Employees Involved with Quality

Train employees to do the job right and then provide statistical sampling techniques and other methods of testing so they can monitor their work in progress. When an employee produces quality work, his or her evaluation and compensation should reflect that success.

Involve employees in the quality program. Ask them about the quality of the goods and services they produce and how the company can do a better job.

Insist on Quality from Suppliers

Everyone needs to be involved in the process of improving quality, including suppliers. When goods are received that do not meet company standards, suppliers should be penalized, while those who delivery quality goods should be rewarded with long-term contracts and preferential bidding. Working with quality-conscious suppliers saves money in more ways than one: Not only does it eliminate delays and repairs incurred by working with inferior components, it also eliminates time spent inspecting subcontractor parts.

Use Customer Feedback for Quality Control

Hertz, the car rental company, instituted a policy of soliciting customer feedback on quality through customer questionnaires. In the process of following up on these suggestions, the company reduced customer complaints to the lowest level in nine years.

Achieve Quality through Automation

Boeing Corporation relies on automation to improve the quality of its product. By computerizing the design, assembly, and inventory control of its aircraft manufacturing operations, the company has made it possible for engineers and assemblers to work together earlier to resolve design-related problems.

Computerization also facilitates the assembly process by ensuring that the right components are on hand at the right time and in the right quantities. As a result of computerization, not only has Boeing improved quality, it has also reduced costly overtime, as well as overhead and rework expenses.

Make Quality Your Trademark

The American Automobile Association is known for its insistence on quality. Its members utilize AAA-certified repair facilities and lodgings because they have come to depend on AAA's recommendation as a guarantee of quality. To receive certification, an establishment must be inspected by field investigators and meet AAA's high standards. In addition, association members who use the services of affiliated establishments are asked to complete a "query card" at the time service work is completed. During one test period, four hundred thousand responses were collected; 96 percent said they were pleased with the quality of service, and 97 percent said they would return to an AAA repair shop.

Clean Up Your Act

A key to quality, and a usually reliable indicator of quality, is a clean workplace. Hammond Berry, a furniture manufacturer, says: "A clean, orderly workplace promotes quality. I can almost sense the extent of a plant's quality level just by walking through and observing their housekeeping."

Berry has another strategy for his own company. "Ever see a plant after it's been straightened up for annual inventory?" he asks. "I used to take pictures which were then used as the 'acceptable standard' for the rest of the year."

Act, Don't React

Like most American auto manufacturers, the Ford Motor Company used to depend on a "reactive" quality-control system that focused on finding and fixing problems after they occurred. Eventually, defects and breakdowns became unacceptable to consumers, especially with the advent of high-quality foreign imports.

To remedy the situation, Ford hired a new quality-assurance director and told him to put the quality back into

Ford. He launched an all-out effort. He organized workers into reliability teams and trained them to understand quality control. Design and assembly engineers worked together to use statistical control techniques to measure production variances. The company introduced a computer-controlled manufacturing system to reduce product variability. Ford even included suppliers in its commitment to quality. With this multifaceted approach, Ford made impressive gains in quality. A nationwide survey showed the number of repairs dropped 59 percent for Ford cars and 47 percent for Ford trucks compared to three years earlier.

When Hewlett-Packard, a high-tech manufacturer, discovered its own lack of quality was raising production costs and product prices, the company took an aggressive five-step approach to the problem.

First, the company set a goal to reduce product failure rates by an ambitious 1,000 percent. Second, managers were trained in quality-assurance techniques. The third step was to train and motivate all employees by setting up more than a thousand quality teams throughout the company. Newsletters, informal meetings, and formal training classes reinforced the quality message. A fourth step involved the installation of a computer system for tracking rework and parts failure. And as a final step, Hewlett-Packard asked its suppliers to establish similar quality goals and to set up their own quality-assurance programs.

In the end, Hewlett-Packard's results were outstanding. The service and repair of desk-top computers decreased 35 percent, while production time also dropped, resulting in lower costs and in some cases lower prices. As a result of its insistence on quality from suppliers, one vendor reduced chip failures to zero over a period of fifteen months. Finally, inventories were reduced over a three-year period from 20.2 percent of sales to 15.5 percent. Translated into sales, Hewlett-Packard had saved $200 million on parts not tied up in inventory.

CHAPTER 5

MEASUREMENT:
How Productive Are You?

Why bother to measure productivity? Because measuring how successful you already are can generate even greater success. Any manager who seeks to improve productivity must find ways to measure results.

Talk to the People Being Measured

Every employee has a sense of how well he or she is doing, and every manager has a feeling about the value of the people he or she manages. These personal assessments are often expressed at work—but not always in a way that seems like a "measurement."

Talking about personal assessments is a first step in developing a useful measurement system. When a manager and an employee agree on what they are trying to accomplish and how they will judge their success, they have developed a productivity measure. Sometimes this process alone will improve productivity, because a worker can find out for the first time what it is the manager really wants.

Look for More than One Measure

Even in the simplest occupations, there is no single instrument that can measure total productivity. Take a straight piecework job, for example, where a worker stamps out parts and is paid at a set rate for each unit produced. You might think that the best measure of productivity would be the number of pieces completed each hour. Although this is certainly one good possibility, other measures are also useful, especially when they can be related to production expenses. Counting the number of unacceptable pieces produced each hour will help incorporate scrap costs, for instance, while calculating the number of pieces produced weekly, instead of hourly, will give an indication of the rate of production over a sustained period of time.

One of the best illustrations of the many ways to measure productivity is our national pastime, baseball. Each year, record books are filled with measures of performance for each player: home runs per game, per inning, per season; batting averages; games played; runs batted in. The statistics are unending. Spome of them may even seem excessive. Nevertheless, these ratings are useful measures in determining how much a player should be paid.

Developing measures to determine compensation is a continuing challenge, and not just in baseball. Prince Corporation, an auto-parts manufacturer, recognizes that no one measure is sufficient, so it has developed a multimeasurement system to assess employee performance and determine pay. Each employee at Prince is given a score of 1 to 5 in five key areas—attendance, quality, quantity, cooperation, and work rules. Hourly wages are determined on the basis of cumulative scores.

All employees at Prince are asked to audit their own work using a standardized quality-rating system. In addition, each worker's output goes through a series of computerized tests, the results of which are posted daily. Both measures give employees an objective evaluation of the quality of their performance and tell them immediately which areas are subject to improvement.

Measure the Intangibles

Measuring the work performance of someone who produces a tangible product is always easier than measuring that of someone in the information or service industry. In fact, there are those who contend that there really is no meaningful way to measure the productivity of a lawyer, an accountant, a floor sweeper, a hotel clerk, or an author.

Participants at a recent meeting of writers and reporters claimed it was impossible to measure effectively the work of people who are concerned with "matters of the intellect." Their product, they said, could only be measured by counting words, and that did not take into consideration the quality of the work. For instance, one reporter had produced eighty-seven stories during the year with an average length of four hundred words, while another reporter had produced only half as many of the same length.

During further discussion, someone commented that it would be interesting to know how many hours each reporter spent on each story, how many stories received prime placement in newspapers and magazines (that is, how many home runs per year), and how many retractions had to be made (that is, number of strikeouts). In the end, most of the participants concluded that although they could think of no comprehensive ways to evaluate the overall productivity of reporters, a variety of useful measurements could be assembled.

No job category is beyond measurement or evaluation. But remember, no single statistic that relates to worker effort should be regarded as an absolute measure of productivity. Numbers and averages cannot be equated with productivity per se in every instance. After all, how can you measure Lincoln's productivity with the Gettysburg Address?

Like editors and reporters, many educators claim their jobs are beyond useful productivity measurement. The ongoing debate over whether teachers should receive merit pay is a productivity issue. The real question is not whether teachers ought to be awarded merit pay, but whether an unbiased system can be devised to evaluate their performance.

Educational institutions have been using productivity measurements for many years, especially in schools of higher learning. Among the criteria used are number of hours taught, number of students in each class, number of publications published, membership on committees, and critiques by colleagues and students.

There are also a number of ways to measure a school's overall productivity, either by creating standardized tests or by mandating statewide examinations. Scores from these exams allow educators to evaluate the change in a students' performance from year to year and to compare the school's performance with those of other institutions.

BEA Associates, a fund management firm, has successfully met the problem of measuring intangible work products. Each BEA fund manager's performance is measured monthly by the return on investment of the funds under his or her management. Portfolios are periodically reviewed for risk and diversification. Yearly performances are analyzed by a research unit that determines where value was added and by whom. Each fund manager is required to study the report and indicate in writing what each manager's compensation should be. Final results are collected and read aloud with individual evaluators remaining anonymous.

Use Technology to Simplify Measurement

Today, computers make it possible to gather and compare productivity data at relatively low cost. General Foods harnessed the power of the computer in an effort to achieve its primary objective—becoming the lowest-cost food producer in the market. To accomplish the feat, a sophisticated system was developed called the Plantwide Productivity Measurement Program. PPMP is composed of individual productivity indexes devised for every facet of every product made by General Foods. Developed from standard cost accounting data, these indexes can be totaled to produce an overall productivity index for each company product or plant. A base-year productivity index was computed by dividing total output by total input. Subsequent output/input calculations are adjusted for inflation. Factors the company includes in measuring output are labor costs per unit of output and materials lost per unit of output. Input factors include direct labor, indirect labor, purchased services and supplies, raw materials, energy, depreciation, property taxes, insurance, and cost of capital. General Foods is identifying production inefficiencies and meeting cost-reduction targets because of PPMP.

Look for Change Over Time

Once you have developed an equitable system for measuring productivity, you will then have the ability to compare your current performance with past results, work performance on one job with work performance for a related activity, one individual's performance with another's, or the performance in one unit or division with that of the rest. Comparing your organization's productivity with industry standards is also useful. Be sure not to overlook the benefits of comparing changes in productivity over time.

Continental Insurance, a domestic property and casualty company with forty branch offices throughout the United States, uses a productivity measurement system called the Productivity Performance Index (PPI) to standardize branch expenses. Before instituting the PPI, the company noticed that branch expenses varied widely from 3 percent to 13 percent of total premium income.

Three different measurements produce PPI. First, to evaluate staffing levels and to compare branch office efficiencies, a Productivity Indicator weighs transactions costs according to difficulty for each processing unit in each branch. Next, the ratio of transactions expenses to premium income is calculated to evaluate relative costs of processing. Finally, service timeliness is measured by computing the average number of days required to process different insurance instruments. When added together, these measurements produce an overall measure of productivity, cost, and effectiveness.

With the PPI pegged to a constant base index, Continental's branch managers can detect changes in productivity at their locations, while the company can compare the performance of one branch with that of another. As a result, productivity has increased throughout the organization. In the first year of using PPI, service levels at Continental rose 12.5 percent, branch expenses dropped 5 percent, and branch offices reduced their staff by 20 percent through attrition and early retirement.

Let Profits Be a Barometer of Productivity

The ultimate measure of any company's productivity and competitiveness is the bottom line, the net profit. It is the ultimate symbol of how well a company is doing—and a reliable indicator of how long it will survive. Return on capital and percentage earnings on sales have become mainstays of financial analysis.

Because productivity contributes to profitability, its measure is an early indicator of any changes that are likely to occur in net income. So if you want to see your profits climb, make sure your productivity is always going up. Productivity measures should be relatively simple, easy to compute, and readily available. After all, measurements are only as good as the use you make of them.

CHAPTER 6

PRODUCTIVE PEOPLE: Harness Your Most Important Resource

Successful managers may argue over technologies and techniques for increasing corporate competitiveness, but they all agree on one crucial point: It is people who make the difference. "We recognize people as our most important asset," begins Dana Corporation's statement of principles. Even the technological giant IBM credits people, not technology, for its incredible growth and record of excellence.

Know the Needs of Your People

Recognizing the integral relationship between people and productivity, competitive edge, and profitability means understanding that today's workers are different from those of past generations. Their educational backgrounds, desires, needs, and attitudes about work have changed. The way they are managed needs to change accordingly.

Traditional methods of management are not always effective in motivating our current generation of workers. Even companies quick to adopt the latest technologies and manufacturing techniques may be late in recognizing the new needs of their people. The result is often a company at odds with itself: a new breed of workers operating in a highly competitive environment, utilizing state-of-the-art technology, but managed by supervisors using the methods and styles of an older generation.

Motivate the New Breed

The competitive challenge for today's managers is to adapt their style to this new breed of worker. A survey conducted by Robert Ranftl, director of managerial productivity for Hughes Aircraft Company, found that personal productivity has little to do with IQ, schools attended, or course grades. What makes the critical difference in a worker's performance, the survey found, is the attitude and motivation of management that are transmitted downward.

How do you motivate this new breed of workers? According to Jerry McAdams, senior manager of Maritz, Inc., an employee benefits advisory firm based in Fenton, Missouri, you have to "create an organization where people share a sense of common fate, not an organization where people have a sense of controlled exchange—money for brawn and brain." According to Barbara Nouveau, director of human resources for the Food Marketing Institute, that means letting people know about the organization in which they work. "They'll have more respect for their company and their job if they understand how the firm works—they might have good ideas as well. The old way of not letting employees in on the inner workings of a company is not valid anymore."

For John Manoogian, Ford Motor Company's director of quality assurance, an effective management style for today requires a good deal of listening. "Why should we reinvent the wheel when our employees already know how to get things rolling?" asks Manoogian. "Listening and responding to suggestions reduces obstacles to raising productivity, profitability, and competitiveness."

Make Employees Part of the Team

Involving workers in the decision-making process and recognizing them for their efforts are critical. "Make people feel that they are part of the team," says Hoyt Parmer, president of Como Plastics. According to Gene Kofke, director of human resources at AT&T, "The one word that will have the greatest impact on labor/management relations and on productivity is recognition."

Becoming more competitive depends on the work force's understanding of one basic principle: An improved competitive position through higher productivity helps everyone. Unfortunately, recent research suggests that managers have not been successful in getting this point across. A 1983 U.S. Chamber of Commerce study indicates that only 9 percent of U.S. workers believe that productivity programs will benefit them personally. Managers must convince their employees that productivity, competitiveness, and profitability are directly related to personal economic status.

Reap the Rewards of People Productivity

There is no one solution for achieving increased people productivity. Success comes from a multitude of strategies: talking to your employees and letting them know your goals; listening to what your people say and letting them know their opinions are valued; acting on employee suggestions and grievances; seeking the cooperation of labor in creating innovative systems; and, finally, recognizing and rewarding those who contribute to your success.

Productivity programs "cost a bundle in time and a bundle in people effort," says Warren Braun, president of ComSonics, "but I tell you, they do work and they work beautifully." Braun should know. Over the past five years, his company has generated a whopping 269 percent increase in sales, earning it a place on *Inc.* magazine's list of the five hundred fastest-growing companies in America.

CHAPTER 7

COMMUNICATION:
A Free Exchange Up and
Down the Organization

No matter how simple it sounds or how often it is heard, it still is absolutely true: Good communication is essential to improving productivity. Employees base their actions on what they think management wants. But too often employee actions are based on incorrect guesses or gossip rather than on accurate information. Yet unless employees know where their company is headed and how it plans to get there, how can they be expected to take the same route or even go in the same direction?

The problem is that most managers think they are adept at communicating when in fact they are not. How can a manager start the communicating process?

"Blue-Sky" the Company

Begin by communicating company goals and policies to every employee. "It's important for employees to know what the company is all about," emphasizes Don Gross, president of Certified Grocers of California. "You have to say it at the top level and mean it all the way down. Every employee has to know he is making a concrete contribution to a defined goal."

When Hughes Aircraft published a brochure, A *Commitment to Productivity*, it was sent to all seventy thousand employees. Says Robert Ranftl, "The brochure spelled out our $1 billion commitment to new technology, and told the employees dollar by dollar how the money would be spent. We solicited their involvement and their commitment to improved productivity. And of greatest importance, we looked to our managers themselves as a key to this entire process. We're trying to develop not only an awareness and an understanding of productivity, but a dedicated commitment to it on the part of our management team."

Share Information

Sharing financial data that were previously held confidential is a strategy recently adopted by Como Plastics. When C. W. Jackson purchased the company in 1980, he brought with him a people-oriented management approach. Now managers meet regularly with production personnel and staff to discuss each month's financial figures.

In addition, Jackson and Hoyt Parmer, the company president, hold a breakfast meeting with twelve or thirteen employees each month. The agenda is wide open. Everything from production techniques and new product lines to retirement benefits and profits is discussed. The results are impressive. Sales at Como Plastics jumped from $8 million to $17 million and profits increased 800 percent.

Learn to Listen and Learn a Lot

For many years Ford strived to improve the way its cars were assembled, but it was common practice, explains chairman Philip Caldwell, to "kick the man downstream who couldn't put the parts together. . . . Eventually we realized that the assemblers might have something to contribute to [solving] the problem." Today, prototype vehicles are taken to the plants where they are to be assembled. Line workers are given the chance to run the process and make suggestions. The benefits are many. Not only does Ford solve its design problems before they can sabotage the assembly process, but workers feel good about their jobs because their suggestions are taken seriously.

"Our employees protect our blind side," explains a manager at a midwestern manufacturing plant. "Who will ask 'what if'? We rely on our people, not our competitors, to do that for us."

Identify the Problem but Let Employees Identify the Solutions

The Westinghouse Nuclear Technology Division recognized that the primary nature of its business was changing from power plant design to engineering product application. This meant its work force would also have to change, because the company no longer needed its high concentration of superstar professionals—3.5 engineers for every technician.

To develop a productivity plan that could estimate future staffing requirements, NTD's management went to its employees and said, "You know our work is changing. Tell us what skills are needed to do your job." Employees were asked to calculate the time they spent on each task and to rate the importance of the tasks in three areas: production, service, and R&D. The survey revealed that 20 to 30 percent of the activities performed by senior engineers could actually be handled by technicians. In addition, engineers told management that they did not like doing work that was not challenging them.

As a result of a concentrated follow-up effort to restructure jobs and establish new hiring requirements, the company was able to lower the ratio of professionals to technicians to 2.7 to 1. The project achieved an 8 percent payroll savings per year. In addition, job satisfaction increased and productivity went up.

Let Employees Wake Up Management

At the Great Salt Lake Minerals and Chemicals Corporation, sleeping on the job was a real problem for workers on rotating shifts. In fact, one-third of the workers at the $37 million-a-year solar pond system reported they could not make it through their eight-hour shift without a nap. The company asked employees to help diagnose and cure the problem. In consultation with the Center for Design of Industrial Schedules at Harvard University, experiments were conducted to find a better shift-rotation system.

By changing shifts every twenty-one days instead of every seven and by rotating shifts forward instead of backward, the problem was greatly diminished. Employees were not only more awake, but more productive, more competitive, and happier. There was a 70 percent decrease in scheduling complaints, as well as a significant decline in employee turnover, absenteeism, and family problems. In the first year of implementing the new schedules, productivity increased 20 percent. "Four years ago," operations manager Preston Richey points out, "our goal was a thousand tons of potash per day; now fifteen hundred tons per day is average with the same work force."

Labor and Management: Share Your Destiny

The presence of a labor union doesn't have to signal the end of communication. It just adds another party to the conversation. Richard Mantia, an official with the St. Louis Building and Construction Trades Council, believes the key to good labor/management relationships lies in both sides recognizing their interdependence. "If we're going to keep the AFL-CIO alive, we have to keep the AFL-CIO contractors in business."

In the seventies, St. Louis had a notorious reputation as a difficult trade union city. Strikes closed construction sites several times a month. Businesses began to defer expansion because of the tense climate. To break the impasse, leaders of the Building and Construction Trades Council sat down with the Associated General Contractors and drew up a "memorandum of understanding" called PRIDE—Productivity and Responsibility Increase Development and Employment. As the title implies, the goal was to increase construction productivity, development, and employment in the St. Louis area. In order to do so, each party had to agree to compromise. The unions eased work rules, eliminated featherbedding, banned jurisdictional strikes, and strengthened on-site management control. In return for a no-picket-line pledge during contract strikes, management agreed to nonbinding arbitration and contractors agreed to hire only union labor.

Because of the PRIDE effort, construction in the St. Louis area quickly went from bust to boom. Trade union members became fully employed, with 98 percent of commercial and 96 percent of residential construction built by AFL-CIO labor. Projects were completed on time and under budget.

PRIDE's example has been successfully copied in at least ten other cities. Included among them are the MOST program (Management and Organized Labor Sticking Together) in Columbus, Ohio, the PEP project (Planning Economic Progress) in Beaumont, Texas, and the Union Jack in Denver, Colorado.

Try Third-Party Facilitators

To keep communication between management and labor open and flowing, a third party is sometimes required. Philip Ray, former director of the Joint Labor Management Committee (JLMC) of the Retail Foods Industry, believes that "a third party can play a valuable role as facilitator between the two sides—making sure they are moving in some direction rather than just stalling."

The JLMC serves this purpose. It convenes meetings for labor and management and serves as a communication clearinghouse. Composed of representatives from the three largest retail food unions, thirteen supermarket companies, and their trade association, the JLMC monitors collective-bargaining negotiations, promotes long-range industry stability, and encourages open communication on industry issues.

Involve the Community

Business, labor, and community leaders in Cleveland, Ohio, revitalized a decaying business community and a bankrupt city. A task force of Cleveland's foremost business, municipal, and civic leaders came together to take a hard look at the city's problems. According to Ruben Mettler, chairman of TRW Inc. and a leading member of the joint effort, the basic problem was the erosion of the community's competitive spirit. Once these leaders committed themselves to competing with foreign and domestic companies, the group was able to chart a steady course for improving productivity and profitability. Cleveland went from bankruptcy to economic renaissance because of communication, cooperation, and commitment.

CHAPTER 8

REWARDS:
Recognize Outstanding
Competitors

How much do you know about employee compensation?
Take a moment to answer these questions:

1. When you work hard and are productive in your job,
do you expect your pay to reflect your success?
2. Does being recognized for a superior performance
make you want to be even more productive?
3. When you spend time and effort increasing your
skills, do you want the company to notice?
4. If you do an outstanding job, do you expect a promotion and additional responsibility?
5. As your company's profits grow, would you like to
share in its financial success?
6. Do you want to participate in company decisions that
affect your job and your future?
7. Does it give you peace of mind to know that as long
as you do your work well, your job is secure?

If you answered yes to every question and if you believe
in the Golden Rule—treating others as you would like to
be treated—then you already know 90 percent of what you

need to know about employee compensation. The rest is detail.

There are many ways—both monetary and nonmonetary—to reward outstanding performance. But the successful managers we interviewed know that two general rules always apply. First, you should use fair and objective standards for determining who is to be rewarded and be sure those standards are well publicized. Second, while there are many types of reward strategies, you should choose the ones specially tailored to the specific needs of your company and the ones your employees really want.

Use Rewards That Work

How do you know what reward will motivate employees best? Just ask them!

That is exactly what Certified Grocers did and found to its surprise that it is not always money. When Certified set up employee/management groups to improve productivity in three key areas—warehouse operations, accounting, and data processing—the warehouse group boldly recommended a nonmonetary reward system. They wanted more time off for above-average performance. With the approval of the union, Certified developed a performance standard based on the amount of work that could reasonably be expected in any job and in any given period of time. Now whenever an employee's production exceeds that standard, that person receives a bonus of paid time off or, if the employee prefers, the monetary equivalent of one-half the time off. One year after installing this new bonus plan, Certified found its production was up more than 15 percent, and the company had saved more than $2 million in payroll costs.

Tie a Bonus to Individual Performance

At Prince Corporation in Holland, Michigan, each of the auto-parts manufacturer's one thousand employees is rewarded individually, with compensation tied to five measurable standards: quantity, quality, work rules, cooperation, and attendance. Although each employee is part of a team, individual pay is based solely on individual performance. This approach has earned Prince top quality ratings from each of the major automakers.

Reward the Group Effort

The Potlatch Corporation, on the other hand, links compensation to group productivity. The billion-dollar producer of wood products developed an hours standard based on the fabrication and packaging of one thousand feet of paneling. When employees work more efficiently, a bonus is paid. If the paneling is produced with a 10 percent savings in hours, for example, the company pays a 10 percent bonus to all line workers. Using this approach, productivity improvement at Potlatch has averaged 5 to 7 percent a year and bonuses have averaged 5 to 8 percent.

Try a Combination of Performance Rewards

At Lincoln Electric, a welding equipment manufacturer, individual and group incentives are combined. Wherever possible, jobs are paid on a piecework basis, so that individual accomplishments can be rewarded. As an additional incentive, the company pays year-end bonuses based on company profits. Lincoln Electric has thrived in this environment and so have its employees. In one year alone, individual bonuses averaged more than $15,000.

Pay for Performance

Paying cash rewards for performance is a proven way for a company to increase its productivity. One form it may take is called "gainsharing." In gainsharing, employees are told in advance what financial rewards they will receive if certain production or profit goals are met. The Participative Management Plan at Motorola is a team approach to gainsharing. Every Motorola employee is a member of a team, and each team is given certain performance goals by a PMP steering committee. For employees involved directly in manufacturing, team goals usually focus on cost, quality, delivery, inventory, housekeeping, and safety standards. Managers, supervisors, and other workers engaged in support positions have goals that emphasize strategic and human resource issues. To qualify for a bonus, a team must meet its goals and its pre-tax profit target. A proportion of the additional profit earned is then paid out in bonuses. Each member's bonus is based on his or her salary's share of the team's total payroll.

Share the Benefits of Higher Quality and Higher Output

Many companies today see the team approach as a way to build competitive spirit. In wage talks with the United Auto Workers (UAW), General Motors proposed that compensation be tied to productivity performance in its individual plants, thereby eliminating across-the-board pay raises for all workers. Although the UAW objected to the proposal, such programs are likely to win out in the future.

For instance, the U.S. Air Force instituted an experimental program at McClellan Air Force Base in California that will tie the pay of two thousand blue-collar workers to team performance. The workers' union, the American Federation of Government Employees, approves in theory the concept of splitting the benefits of higher quality and higher output. The employees can expect better wages, while the employer—Uncle Sam—can expect to get a better job done at a lower cost.

Make Employees Owners

When workers become owners, they take new interest in the health of their firm and usually do a better job. They think not only about today, but also about what is good for the long-term future of the company. "Employee ownership plans," says Lowe's chairman Robert Strickland, "are the most dynamic and most flexible gainsharing plans. They combine two very powerful forces—economics and human nature. When done correctly, they are seedbeds for motivation and productivity."

Strickland further explains, "In the late fifties and early sixties, there were at least five retail companies in the Sunbelt just like ours—same geography, same business, different management, of course, but not bad management. Three of the companies didn't make it on their own and sold out. The fourth company, which is about one-fourth our size, has just adopted an ESOP. The fifth company, without an ESOP, has had a mediocre record." Since adopting its own employee ownership plan in the late 1950s, Lowe's has grown from six stores to 205 in nineteen states, and its sales volume has increased fifty times over. By 1983, Lowe's sales-per-employee figures were three times the average for the big-three retailers (Sears, K mart, and J. C. Penney), all non-employee-owned businesses.

Lowe's has found employee ownership to be a powerful motivator for those groups that are often the most difficult to motivate—young middle managers and low-income, blue-collar workers. "Now our aggressive young store managers check on their wealth every weekday by looking up Lowe's in the New York Stock Exchange," says Strickland. Blue-collar workers are motivated by the possibility of retiring with a big nest egg. They look to the example of one Lowe's employee who had never earned more than $125 a week but who retired with $660,000 worth of Lowe's stock.

Ten years ago, few companies could see the benefits of employee stock ownership programs because the concept was so foreign to the traditional owner/employee relationship. During the last decade, however, the popularity of ESOPs has grown dramatically. More than four thousand plans are now in place. In addition, another four thousand companies have alternative forms of stock bonus and employee ownership programs.

According to the National Center for Employee Ownership, ESOPs have had a positive impact on productivity and competitiveness. After examining forty-five companies that used ESOPs over a ten-year period, the Center reported that sales in these companies grew about 5½ percent a year faster than did the sales in their non-ESOP competitors.

Use Stock Options and Bonuses

Stock option and bonus plans are also ways to make employees part owners of the business. These types of plans allow managers to reward employees at reduced cost to the company. A stock bonus program substitutes company stock for cash bonuses. A stock option program provides benefits similar to those of a stock bonus plan, but instead of transferring stock to an employee immediately, it gives the employee the option of purchasing stock at some time in the future at a price fixed at the time the option is granted.

Pay for Skills

Rewarding employees for acquiring new skills and knowledge can help solve a multitude of management problems. Pay-for-skills programs provide new challenges and opportunities for employees. They reduce employee turnover by eliminating dead-end jobs that force employees to look elsewhere for new challenges and they offer incentives for employees to stay on their jobs.

Most important, a pay-for-skills plan allows employees to do what they do best. A top-flight physicist, for instance, can continue to do laboratory work and does not have to accept a management position just to earn more money; this scientist's income will increase as he or she acquires more technical knowledge. The company avoids losing an excellent researcher—and also avoids the expense of recruiting a replacement. At the same time, the company can fill its management positions with people who are better suited to be managers than are scientists.

Increase Personnel Flexibility

Companies like Procter & Gamble have found that pay-for-skills plans increase their flexibility. "We decided to pay people a weekly salary determined by the number of different jobs an individual can perform," explains Stanley Holditch, a former P&G manager. Under P&G's system, employees are divided into work groups. As group members learn each other's jobs, their rates of pay are increased. Once an employee learns all the functions performed in one group, he or she then goes on to learn the functions of another group. Cross-training allows workers to cover for one another in case of illness, or fill in when a key employee leaves the company. It also smooths the apprenticeship of new employees, since everyone is knowledgeable enough to assist in the training. In addition, workers gain greater job security. They can easily be moved to another position if their job becomes obsolete.

Eliminate Dead-End Jobs

For the police department in Palantine, Illinois, the adoption of a pay-for-skills program, called the Dual Career Ladder (DCL), provided the solution to a low-morale problem caused by too few promotion opportunities. Before DCL, officers had to wait for the death or retirement of a superior before they could advance. DCL solved the problem by redesigning the traditional career ladder. Police personnel are now able to earn more money and receive greater recognition just by acquiring new skills.

Palatine's deputy chief of police, Walter Gasior, is enthusiastic about the multiple benefits of the program. "It improves their capabilities as professionals, enhances their performance as police officers, and maximizes overall performance of the department," he says. "What's more, it provides cost-effective police service to the community." Since DCL was installed, Palatine has been able to reduce the total number of police personnel it employs, while at the same time increasing overall departmental productivity by 10 percent.

Promote Job Security

More and more companies are finding that job security is a primary concern of their employees. In many instances, it has replaced pay and benefits as the principal bargaining issue between companies and labor unions. Fordham University business professor Marta Mooney believes employment security is of greatest concern to middle managers. They have the most difficulty locating new jobs if laid off, and they are first to go when management layers have to be sacrificed.

The ultimate reward may be a secure job. "Some say full employment is a luxury only a company like ours can afford," says a senior IBM personnel officer. "Maybe we can afford it because we make the commitment, and because our people respond to that commitment with a business performance that makes it affordable. Concern for full employment—indeed, job security—is the very foundation of increased productivity. By using their minds as well as their hands, our people have cut two-thirds of the hours that go into manufacturing our product. The cost of the product went down 45 percent during a ten-year period when wages vastly increased. That achievement would have been impossible without productive and committed employees. And much of their commitment stems from the security they know is theirs."

How do you develop a job-security program? Here are a few guidelines from companies that have successfully taken the plunge:

1. Adopt a formal corporate policy demonstrating a commitment to employment security. Lincoln Electric, for example, guarantees all permanent, full-time employees a maximum of thirty hours of work a week for forty-nine weeks a year. Lincoln has always honored its commitment, even during the 1981–1982 recession.

2. Hire and promote from within the company as much as possible. At Digital Equipment Corporation all hiring from outside the company must be approved by a senior vice-president.

3. Train and retrain employees in new skills to increase their job mobility within the firm.

4. Maintain a lean permanent work force that can be augmented, as needed, with planned overtime or temporary workers. At IBM, overtime, contract suppliers, and temporary personnel are used during periods of peak production. "A buffer strategy is an important part of the planning process," says one IBM official, "because it means that if the work load falls short of expectations, for any reason, we can decrease overtime, reduce temporary assignments, or limit the work we vend to ensure full-time work for all our regular employees."

5. Guarantee continuity of employment by obtaining a commitment from employees or their union representatives for increased flexibility in job assignments, training, and relocation. When McCreary Tire & Rubber Company in Indiana, Pennsylvania, fell victim to a recession, management worked with employees to establish a work-furlough program. As an alternative to laying off a third of the work force, McCreary allowed each employee to work two weeks out of three during the summer, while it investigated additional cost-cutting measures and switched production from low-demand passenger car tires to high-margin truck and specialty tires. The state of Pennsylvania also agreed to pay supplemental unemployment benefits for the weeks employees were on furlough.

As a result, the company's payroll costs were reduced significantly while productivity rose, absenteeism fell, and on-the-job injuries decreased. McCreary not only weathered the recession but emerged a lot stronger. "The payroll savings helped us through a tough time, and kept everyone on the job," a personnel supervisor observes. "We've been notorious in the last few years for losing money, but now we're a profitable firm."

The Ford Motor Company and the United Auto Workers set up a program jointly administered by the company and the union to help retrain workers whose jobs had become endangered. Established under a collective-bargaining agreement, the UAW-Ford Employee Development and Training Program (EDTP) is funded by a Ford contribution of five cents per worker hour.

The EDTP encompasses four key areas: educational training and assistance; national vocational retraining assistance; targeted vocational retraining; and career counseling and guidance. At present, over 1,300 active Ford employees participate in EDTP, which provides money for tuition at approved institutions, and 4,500 furloughed employees are taking advantage of the National Vocational Retraining Assistance Plan, which pays for courses related to the automotive and other industries. The Targeted Vocational Retraining Project helps over 650 laid-off employees receive technical training in occupations with immediate job opportunities, while over 2,000 furloughed employees have graduated from the Career Counseling and Guidance Program.

Promote Job Satisfaction

Experts say a worker's greatest reward is job satisfaction. Keeping employees satisfied means constantly providing new challenges and new and different responsibilities. One challenge that workers always seem eager to meet is participatory decision-making. "The art of creating participation is a reward in itself," notes Irving DeToro of Xerox. "It allows for achievement, learning, and mastery over one's environment. These rewards, in turn, can serve as powerful motivators for the achievement of organizational goals."

Include Employees in Decision-making

According to Ron Contino, deputy commissioner for support operations for New York City's Department of Sanitation, "The process of getting labor involved in the running of an operation is not only exciting and rewarding, it's also extremely worthwhile in terms of improving productivity and service quality."

When Contino took over departmental operations in 1978, the Bureau of Motor Equipment was widely recognized as being in a state of chaos. Almost half its sanitation trucks were inoperative on any given day, the amount of overtime was extraordinarily high, and substantial "rework" was constantly required. To turn the bureau around, Contino gave employees greater control over their work environment by allowing them to participate in development, management, procurement, and budget programs. Repair and collection crews became involved in the evaluation of new equipment and worked with supervisors in establishing the specifications for collection vehicles. Equipment design and manufacture of repair parts were done in-house. The result: reduced part costs while inventory levels are still maintained. Today, the bureau's repair shops are operating at a "profit-center" productivity level. In fact, every dollar the city invests in its operation has been calculated to be worth $1.41 in goods and services purchased from the private sector.

Enhance Job Responsibility

Fab Steel, which fabricates petrochemical plant steel superstructures, has successfully expanded employee responsibility through its Triangle of Responsibility Program for managers. The "Triangle" concept broadens managerial focus in three ways: on their own principal tasks, on overall company competitiveness, and on helping one another in different parts of the company. Champion International encourages increased responsibility and better management through its "Managing for Excellence" program, which trains "high-potential" managers in finance and human resource development.

Find the Perfect Mix

Some companies find a single program of rewards sufficient but most find it takes a combination of incentives to motivate employees. Amway, the direct sales company, developed a sophisticated reward and recognition system to motivate its independent distributors, who number more than a million. Distributors earn commissions based on the retail product sales they make. They also receive commissions—and performance bonuses—based on the income generated by the new salespeople they sponsor. Since a sponsoring distributor is responsible for paying his or her team members their performance bonus when they in turn sponsor others, the fortunes of distributors and sponsors are inextricably linked. Employees are rewarded for their individual efforts as well as for those of their group. Of course, nothing is paid unless a sale is made, because at Amway sales are the name of the game.

Amway distributors are recognized in nonmonetary ways as well. As sales volume increases, they become eligible for awards and designations—pins, plaques, trips, and cars. Anytime anyone achieves a new sales plateau, a profile of that person is featured in *Amagram*, the company magazine. These incentives seem to be producing the desired result: Amway sales, which totaled $500,000 in 1959, have grown to almost $2 billion today.

Rewarding employees should be seen not as a way of buying allegiance, but as a way of demonstrating management's concern for its people. After all, when you are facing competition on a global scale, it pays to have team members who are committed to a common cause, rather than mercenaries who are committed only to themselves.

CHAPTER 9

INVESTMENT: Capitalize on New Technology and Research

We are a country of inventors, innovators, and entrepreneurs. It has been said, "The U.S. can out-invent the rest of the world combined." So far, we still do. Unfortunately, American companies in recent years have failed to apply this inventiveness to their products, services, and marketing. For example, the VCR is an American invention. Yet when American companies decided not to pursue the market opportunity, the Japanese developed it. The challenge to American businesses today is to regain control of their heritage of inventiveness and technology.

Keeping up-to-date on new manufacturing or service techniques is a primary responsibility of management. Making sure that new investments in offices and plants embody the right technology is the second step. The third step is teaching employees to use their new tools effectively.

Overcome Any Fears of Technology

Payoffs through technology require a level of awareness by all managers and employees. To develop this awareness, you must first overcome any fears of technology. Begin by

developing programs to make technology better under-
stood and less threatening. General Electric conquers
"technophobia" by setting up new robotics equipment in
employee lunchrooms. In this nonthreatening environment, workers see, touch, and play with new equipment.
Without pressure, they discover why it is to their advantage
to adopt new technologies.

Some workers resist automation because they think it
will make their jobs obsolete. When this happens, it is management's responsibility to show workers how technology
can actually save their jobs by making their company more
competitive. General Electric faced this challenge when it
decided to automate its seventy-year-old locomotive plant
in Erie, Pennsylvania, with new computer-controlled machine tools and computer-aided design, engineering, and
manufacturing systems. Automation did reduce the number of workers required to produce each locomotive, but
the total number of jobs in Erie actually increased because
the lower prices that resulted from automation increased
the demand for GE trains.

Glen Watts, retired president of the Communication
Workers of America, once opposed technology—until he
saw what it could do for his union members. He even resisted the introduction of dial telephones at first, because
he thought they would put operators out of work. Of
course, the new technology made telephoning so inexpensive that, within a few years, the volume of calls dramatically outstripped the available pool of operators. In fact, if
all calls were still operator-assisted today, the services
needed would far exceed the industry's ability to provide
them—even if every person in America were to become an
operator!

Plant the Seeds of Technological Awareness

TRW, the multibillion-dollar electronics manufacturer,
learned the value of "seeding" technological awareness at
every level when it had to wrestle with problems in its own
internal communications network. Because the company

had worked hard to foster technological awareness, it turned to its own people to solve the problems it was facing.

The company first convened an internal management problem-solving group, one of whose members suggested an electronic mail and message system. Another task force defined the company's needs. After conferring with an outside firm that specialized in system installation TRW chose a word-processing and electronic mail system that instantly interfaces all parts of the company. Each division within TRW can now maintain its own electronic bulletin board, standardize communications lists for simultaneous delivery to managers throughout the world, edit and forward new messages, and reroute incoming messages. As a result of the new technology, the time it takes TRW managers to make decisions has been slashed by 50 percent. Company telephone costs have been cut 15 percent and overall communications productivity has improved.

Stay Ahead of the Technology Curve

The accelerated rate of technological change today challenges even high-technology leaders. The makers of integrated circuit boards, for example, introduce new chips almost annually, and sales and market shares are won by those who offer the most powerful and the least expensive. In such a ruthless competitive environment, today's winner can easily become tomorrow's loser.

Honeywell had to struggle with the issue of high-tech obsolescence when it failed to direct its technological antenna inward. The company's own field operations were burdened with an inefficient system for internal communications. The company found itself in the curious position of having to use systems for word processing, data communications, the remote entry of sales and accounting information, and the transmission of information to regional networks that were not as up-to-date or efficient as those it provided to its own customers.

An internal service organization was commissioned by senior management to survey the company's needs, and in the end it recommended the development and installation of the Office Administrative Support and Information System (OASIS), which now provides Honeywell with integrated communications services. Because of OASIS, Honeywell expects a return of 20 percent each year on its initial $5 million investment. As an added benefit, the company has a new and well-tested system it can market to its customers.

Companies like Bell Atlantic, Softool, and Federal Express are working to make sure they will not be caught off guard by new technology. By investing in research and development and by using a capital investment strategy consistent with the current market, they are staying ahead of the technology curve and reaping healthy profits as well.

By developing cellular phone technology, Bell Atlantic thought it could apply an old concept to a new market—people who used their cars for offices like salesmen and delivery men. Realizing this new market could contribute significantly to its future growth, the company made investment in this area a high priority. Advertising efforts were geared to showing businesses how cellular telephones could make employees more productive. When customers were ready to buy, Bell Atlantic had the new product already on the shelves.

Softool decided to capitalize on the irony of the automators being unautomated. It uses computers and special software to aid in the development and management of computer software systems. Controlling new versions and revisions of software, data, graphics, and ordinary text will be less monumental with the aid of the computer used to generate them. Softool has targeted that opportunity.

From the beginning, Federal Express saw that the value in the service it provided was the quick transmission of information—not just paper and packages—from one point to another. The overnight mail system it developed in 1973 depended, in part, on the computerized control of information, which has assured almost 100 percent reliability in delivery. A forward-thinking concept, made affordable through technology, became an overwhelming success for Federal Express.

Unfortunately for Federal Express, the company's ZAP mail service fizzled after an uninspiring launch. Federal Express failed to realize that companies with a need to transmit written communications quickly would rather invest in telefax equipment themselves. Even companies that aggressively try to anticipate and cultivate the needs of their customers sometimes fail.

Develop a Technology-Awareness Program

Here are some strategies you can use to reap the benefits of new technologies:

1. Make developing and adopting new ways of doing things an explicit company objective. If you emphasize this approach consistently, it is sure to become a part of your corporate culture and employees will work at finding improvements.

2. Let all employees know what new ideas are under development by the company, its suppliers, its customers, and its competitors. You may not need state-of-the-art equipment, but you should be aware of what is available.

3. Provide technical journals, trade magazines, and other materials for employees. Hold your people responsible for keeping up-to-date on technological developments in their area.

4. Train all employees in the use of computers. Once an intimidated employee has had even rudimentary hands-on experience, fears and inhibitions will quickly dissipate.

5. Find out about government programs that assist companies in identifying available technology. The Pennsylvania Technical Assistance Program, for example, directs companies toward the kind of technological information that will help them stay competitive. The Federal Laboratory Consortium also disseminates information helpful to businesses in developing new products and processes.

Survive World-Class Competition with New Technology

General Electric has met the foreign challenge—you can too! Facing stiff and growing competition, GE realized it had only three choices: automate, emigrate (offshore), or evaporate. In GE's dishwasher division, for example, foreign-made machines were infiltrating an already highly competitive domestic market. GE knew the real problem was its own: Its high-volume production system was obsolete, and competitors were able to underprice GE by relying on innovative "just-in-time" production methods. Instead of warehousing large inventories, as did GE, the competition used computers to schedule parts and supply deliveries to arrive "just in time" for last-minute assembly.

Refusing to evaporate, GE began to invest in high-tech automation and production redesign. The company developed a just-in-time, point-of-use manufacturing system in which computer-controlled machines assemble parts on an as-needed basis at a location close to the main assembly line. In assembling the tub units for GE dishwashers, for example, four punch presses each make a different part of the tub. The dishwasher control panels are produced at an adjacent location and, when complete, are automatically placed on a conveyor belt and moved about fifty feet to where computer-controlled machines attach them to the tub units. Robots then place the completed tub on an overhead conveyor, and in this manner a tub is completed every ten seconds. Quality control is handled by yet another computer, which will not allow production to continue if a unit is not properly assembled. The system is flexible enough to accommodate product modifications, allowing GE to adapt to changing consumer needs.

GE's bold investment in new technology has paid off handsomely. The new system substantially reduced inventory and production expenses at the dishwasher plant. Labor, materials, and overhead costs were cut 10 percent. Overall productivity increased 25 percent and product quality improved as well. In fact, eighteen months after instituting the new system, consumer warranty complaints on GE dishwashers declined 53 percent. Most important, GE has kept its customers, its position in the marketplace, and a profitable product line.

Make Technology Work for You

Successful companies like GE recommend the following strategies to companies who want to make technology work for them:

1. Be sure company objectives go beyond just technological awareness. Look for obstacles that have crept into your policy and operating manuals. Change those things you think may impede technology.

2. Reevaluate your proposed capital acquisitions against what the market has to offer that is new. Buy what you already have only if nothing else is available.

3. Design your service or product line and your production operations to maximize the use of technology. Do not force new technology onto an old way of doing things.

4. Automate in stages if you cannot automate an entire process.

5. Integrate people and machines. Involve employees from the beginning. Provide adequate training so employees will use and maintain their equipment properly.

6. Above all, plan for the long term. Work with local high schools and colleges. Let them know the technical skills you need and allow them to become familiar with your equipment. Tell them about the educational deficiencies that you think are impeding your productivity.

Pool Technological Resources

Pool your resources with other organizations, if necessary, to take advantage of technological breakthroughs. For example, eight small businesses got together a few years ago to form the Small Business Technology Group, Inc., to bid on contracts to construct high-technology systems. Their first customer was the Air Force Electronics Systems Division and Development Center. Alone, none of the companies could have met the bidding requirements of the Air Force, nor did any one company have all the know-how to develop the desired electronics system. By collectively sharing both risks and rewards, they succeeded. Now they aggressively seek out new clients for their technological talents.

Jack Rennie, a founder of the Small Business Technology Group, approaches big production opportunities boldly. "A lot of times the government would rather grant a single multifunction contract. This has the effect of cutting out small businesses, because they can't qualify as the primes." By pooling resources, he notes, little companies can still go after the big contracts.

The strategy of pooling resources is not limited to small companies. Rather than lamenting the government support for computer development in Japan, William Norris, chairman of Control Data Corporation, decided to fight back. He recruited six major computer companies to form Microelectronics Computer Corporation (MCC). Its goal is to tackle the development of next-generation computers. With the combined resources of its members, MCC can afford to fund the kind of basic research that will help assure U.S. supremacy in the supercomputer race.

Forming a research and development limited partnership (RDLP) is another way resources and knowledge can be combined to tackle innovations that are too much for one company to handle. An RDLP pools the financial and sometimes technical resources of several investors or participants to support an R&D effort. If the effort succeeds and a new technology, production process, or product results, the investors receive a payback from its sale or licensing. In addition, an investing partner may have a special right to license the technology for use in its own company, which enables it to acquire a technology made possible through a joint effort. The partnership may also be structured in such a way that one company obtains exclusive use of the technology and pays the others for its use.

Genentech Inc., an innovator in genetic engineering, used this approach when it was faced with a pressing need to raise capital. The company considered licensing its new human growth hormone (HGH) and gamma-interferon technology to a foreign country, but instead it decided to raise $55 million through an RDLP and share the profits from its HGH technology with some outside investors. In this way, Genentech was able to retain control over its new product, preserve its equity ownership, and still raise enough money to see its innovation through to FDA approval.

Cooperation has never been customary in the garment industry. Highly labor intensive, it is also an industry that has traditionally designed and used capital equipment for individual tasks such as folding, cutting, or sewing. Few attempts were made to upgrade this technology until foreign competition forced manufacturers to choose between moving their plants overseas or taking strategic action.

Some clothing companies chose to fight back by forming the Tailored Clothing Technical Corporation. Using its joint funding, they were able to work with Draper Laboratory to develop new robotic sewing systems. Now in place, these systems are reducing manufacturing costs for men's apparel throughout the country. The companies and unions that make up the corporation are confident they may finally have found a way to give America's hard-hit garment industry a competitive edge.

Use Technology to Sharpen Your Competitive Edge

Distribute Computer Controls throughout Your Company. General Motors uses a distributed computer control (DCC) system to direct the different functions in its manufacturing process. Recently, GM improved its DCC operations by making all its computer-controlled systems capable of communicating with each other. As an example of how its factories of the future will work, GM demonstrated how work stations designed by twenty-five different

computer equipment manufacturers could be intercon-
nected so that machines, computers, and people can all
communicate directly. GM plans to extend the system to
suppliers and retail sales networks as well. DCC systems
are expensive—Exxon Chemical Company spent $500,000
installing a DCC system that controls temperatures, pres-
sures, and raw materials flow in its chemical reactors. But
Exxon thinks the system is worth the cost and expects to
recoup its initial investment in only two years.

Perform Repetitive Tasks Error Free. Another technological breakthrough is the computer numerically controlled
(CNC) system, which helps manufacturers produce complex parts and products. Huron Machine Products found
that the initial cost of its CNC equipment could be easily
recovered because, once programmed, its machines do not
have to be set, tested, and reset. One Huron employee can
easily operate several machines simultaneously. The CNC
system has improved safety conditions and lowered labor
costs for Huron.

Eliminate Guesswork. Amcast Industrial Corporation of
Dayton, Ohio, is now able to eliminate the guesswork and
make steel production a lot easier by using computer systems to monitor and record all the conditions necessary to
producing good steel. Amcast is now competitive with all
foreign steel imports.

Customize Products to Customer Orders. Deere & Company integrated its CNC equipment with a DCC system to
produce a flexible manufacturing system (FMS) that can
customize products for specific clients easily and inexpensively.

Match Manufacturing and Assembly. Parts unavailability
and the incorrect sequencing of assembly line processes
used to result in production delays at Boeing ranging from
four hours to four days on a single plane. Now a computerized scheduling and inventory control system automati-

cally chooses the optimal assembly sequence and assures parts availability. By eliminating overtime and overhead resulting from production delays, Boeing has improved both its productivity and profitability. Similarly, General Electric found that installing a production scheduling system at its Wilmington, North Carolina, aircraft plant has increased productivity 30 percent, while achieving a 30 to 40 percent reduction in inventory expenses.

Reduce Inventory Costs. Humana Inc., a large for-profit health organization, found that a computerized inventory control system allows it to benefit from economies of scale by controlling purchasing for its seventeen-thousand-bed acute-care facilities. Humana estimates that it saved $85 million in three years.

General Electric was considering abandoning its meter production plant in Somersworth, New Hampshire, because it was running out of room. Instead, the company built an addition on the roof and designed a materials-handling system that makes the multi-level facility as efficient as a single-floor plant. GE used computers to integrate the storage and inventory systems at Somersworth and converted the space above the production floor to a storage facility. The manufacturing system is now connected by conveyor networks to the forty-thousand-square-foot storage system overhead. "The dog had learned new tricks," says Jules Mirabel, a GE technology manager. "We moved in computers, lasers, robots, and a highly advanced materials-handling system. It's still an old-looking building from the outside, but inside those meters are pouring out."

Make the Computer Serve the Customer. J. C. Penney recognized early on the part computers could play in retailing. During the 1960s it pressed suppliers to install point-of-sales terminals so that it could control inventory, identify customer buying patterns, and better respond to customer needs. A competitor, Sears, Roebuck and Co., found that information stored in its computer system could help it "cross-sell" services. As a new-product warranty nears expiration, for example, the Sears system generates a letter to the customer to recommend an extended warranty contract.

As a manager, none of your responsibilities is more important than knowing how to choose and use the right technology. Invest the time and energy to understand and use this capital resource. It is an unending challenge, but one that can keep your company a successful and profitable competitor.

CHAPTER 10

AMERICA ON THE MOVE

America has extraordinary and abundant economic resources. It has created a technological base that is unsurpassed in size, a skilled labor force, unparalleled opportunities for education and training, and vast capital markets. It provides a competitive advantage that is there for the taking. The challenge now is to use these resources to regain our position as the preeminent, world-class competitor.

Among America's greatest assets is our free-market system, which allows the constant creation of new enterprises and new jobs. In 1988 and 1989, for example, over six hundred thousand new companies were formed in the United States each year, and from November 1982 through August 1989 about twenty million new jobs were created.

Our economic freedom, which gives us the flexibility to move about, to change careers and employers, and to make our own luck, surpasses that of any other country in the world. This freedom is more than a theoretical concept. It gives entrepreneurs and employees the right to choose where they work and, in greater measure than anywhere else, with whom they work. And it also gives employers a tremendously diverse pool of talent.

The freedom to associate and to form new enterprises is

the essence of the entrepreneurial spirit in America; it is just easier to conceive and start a new business here than in other countries. Knowing this helps make Americans more creative by nature and stimulates a greater degree of entrepreneurial behavior.

New smaller businesses are large contributors to productivity and job creation. They arise because their founders believe they can reap the rewards of becoming superior competitors. Existing businesses can take advantage of that initiative in many ways: by allowing new companies to grow within existing companies, by capitalizing entrepreneurs and promoting their ideas, and by developing new services and products for larger markets.

The freedom to compensate and reward at will (instead of according to mandated plans, as is common in many other countries) gives U.S. employers the right to choose those incentives they think will best motivate their people. Being able to provide job security programs without being compelled to do so by the government, for example, makes such programs seem like a reward to workers rather than an entitlement.

Profit-sharing and stock ownership plans are also more attractive in the United States because of the opportunities here to start, build, and expand companies. The breadth of capital and securities markets makes employee ownership a more viable alternative. Traditionally a nation of owners rather than renters, we Americans are more receptive to ownership motivation. And because of our relatively classless society, we often can and do aspire beyond our current station because we know that social barriers can be easily overcome. When a work force is just waiting to meet the competition and is eager to win, managers need only to know how to open the starting gates.

The greatest American advantage is our free, competitive society and its ability to create a productive environment. Economic freedom is at the root of the American heritage, and it can be a supremely valuable asset in becoming more productive, more competitive, and more profitable.

We Have the Capital

America's capital markets are the largest and, more important, the most efficient in the world. Money is available here to support creative ideas and innovative technology, which are the lifeblood of healthy competition. In the last five years, initial public stock offerings have raised $65 billion for their companies, and established firms have raised $87 billion by selling additional shares. That means that more than $152 billion in new funds have been available to promote new ideas, build new plants, buy new equipment, fund new product lines, and pay off debts—all of which are essential ingredients to becoming more competitive. And even more money awaits offshore, as foreign capital markets continue to supply our growth.

Some businesses have taken advantage of this capital in ways that have led them to higher levels of growth and profitability. But other businesses have had to learn the hard way that management's failure to use capital productively can result in losing the competitive edge. The many cases of companies that elected not to use their capital assets to modernize and grow are well known. A good example within the copper industry is Anaconda Copper, which has substantially left the business, while Phelps Dodge has used its capital to develop a new process that cut the cost of producing copper by 50 percent. Anaconda went another route that led it to the evaporation point. Phelps Dodge has grown to become the largest and most competitive U.S. copper producer. Another example is Nucor Steel's use of continuous casting to outcompete much larger companies such as U.S. Steel. A long list of steel companies went out of business because they failed to spend their capital on the new technologies. But unfortunately, we know only anecdotally the names of those small ventures that made good use of capital markets to raise funds for productive enterprise.

While the future of American business is in the hands of individual competitors, government can play a role by providing an economic environment that allows for the raising and managing of capital to the best advantage. If the government provides a stable economy with low inflation, individual businesses can maximize efficiency and capital management.

We Have the Knowledge

The United States is unparalleled in the abundance of information it provides people about inventions, innovations, new technologies, and new techniques. Universities, government research laboratories, business enterprises, and productivity centers are all storehouses of knowledge on how to improve productivity and profits. And most of this information is freely available to anyone who wants to know about it. Unfortunately, many people think that what is free has little value.

Most government research centers are open to the public, and their scientists are usually eager to help companies in need. Many have also discovered brilliant solutions to nagging business problems—solutions that are only waiting to be picked up by a company willing to bring them to market. Still, the "not-invented-here" syndrome keeps most companies away from federal labs. Also, there are even greater opportunities awaiting those who will just take the time to look—and the variety is infinite, from flat-panel displays to devices that can measure the amount of lean meat in ground beef. Either technology could make a clever entrepreneur a handsome return by carving out a premier market niche.

America is truly the invention capital of the world. And over 90 percent of the new knowledge that becomes available each year comes from government- and industry-sponsored research, which government offices and educational institutions are only too willing to share. Many also provide clearinghouses to disseminate the kind of information about technology, productivity, and the characteristics of successful businesses that would be helpful to the competition-minded manager.

We Have the Competitors

There is a lot of talk these days about unfair competition and unlevel playing fields. There is no doubt about it: World competition is not always fair, and can sometimes be brutal. So when you are trying to compete, you had better be willing to use all the resources at your disposal: people, technology, the commitment to quality, and basic American ingenuity. Fighting to win means using everything you've got.

In recent years American companies have become accustomed to competing within the national economy according to generally accepted rules and guidelines. Now they must learn to compete in a world market without such codes of conduct. Yet this is nothing really new in the American experience. Certainly, our earliest days produced some rough and tough competitors. Once again, we need to return to our roots, to those competitive techniques and strategies that made America great.

We Have the Diversity

In this world economy where we must all now compete, the diversity of the American people may turn out to be one of our greatest natural assets. Because of it, all the different talents of the world—every race, creed, nationality, religion, and culture—are available within our borders. Employers can draw from this diverse pool of backgrounds and talents in selecting their work forces and finding the special experts that will help them become sharpshooters.

Some will cite the Far East as an example in arguing that ethnic uniformity always gives a country a competitive edge. But all the evidence seems to suggest that even Japan's phenomenal success is more a result of economic necessity than any other single factor. Indeed, most of Japan's technological advances do not stem from its homogeneity but, rather, from the careful observations it has made of its American ally. While a common ethnic and religious heritage may have its advantages, the energy and competitive spirit created in a diverse America have far outweighed the benefits of uniformity in the past. If we can learn to take advantage of these strengths now, we can use them to win again in the future.

We Have the American Advantage

America offers many other advantages that also foster competitiveness. It has the world's largest consumer market, the most extensive and sophisticated communications systems, a free press, a massive and universal education system, an extensive transportation network, an expansive heartland that supplies food and natural resources, and, above all, a heritage of innovation, social mobility, and entrepreneurial spirit.

Sometimes we forget about this heritage, or simply take it for granted. But most visitors from abroad who spend some time in the United States are inevitably surprised to find the country so extraordinarily class-free and democratic, its people daring to think great thoughts. Even the Swiss, Japanese, and Germans, renowned as tireless workers, are amazed at how hard Americans work and how economically and socially mobile we are. Here, everyone has the chance to pursue the highest goals, even though we may not all begin at the same starting line or achieve the same degree of success. And the stigma of failure is greatly diminished because most Americans are truly forgiving: Starting over again at a new job or setting up yet another new business is always a possibility. Such attitudes stimulate productive activity and competition.

All has not been perfect in the U.S. business environment in recent years. We have often lost ground to competitors from abroad. But we are recapturing that ground because it is still possible to use America's natural and man-made advantages to our benefit in becoming more successful competitors. The techniques and strategies of good management we have described in the previous pages can be adapted and applied across the board to improve productivity in any company. The corporate case studies in the pages that follow show how many American companies have implemented these strategies with dramatic success. Economic freedom, ingenuity, and the enterprise of the American people are the elements common to all their stories. We have only to follow their lead to regain our competitive edge and secure our future success.

PART II

COMPANIES THAT ARE
MAKING IT HAPPEN

CORPORATE CASE STUDIES IN PRODUCTIVITY: An Overview

Allegheny Ludlum Corporation
Computerized cost-measurement system, aided by nonfunction-alized management organization, helps achieve 45 percent productivity improvement

America West Airlines
New national carrier combines employee stock ownership, job cross-utilization, fuel-efficient aircraft, and a hub city operation to achieve high employee morale and productivity

America Seating Company
Cost-reduction teams use committee process to set productivity goals and provide the plans and operating leadership to achieve them

Amway Corporation
Dual-opportunity reward system motivates independent sales distributors and helps company achieve $1.9 billion in sales

Apple Computer, Inc.

Just-in-time inventory control and materials flow systems provide improved quality, increased productivity, and lower cost in high-tech manufacturing plant

The Bank of New York

Bank's statistical quality-control procedures lower error rates by as much as 70 percent

BEA Associates, Inc.

Fund management firm retains key money managers and achieves spectacular growth through participative compensation and centralized operational support

Beatrice Companies, Inc.

Giant manufacturer installs total productivity program at 150 profit centers and achieves $50 million in savings

Calvert Group

Computerized telephone system creates satisfied customers for financial services organization

Certified Grocers of California Ltd.

Labor/management plan rewards more productive warehouse workers with time off and extra pay

Champion International

$4 billion conglomerate develops corporate philosophy of employee involvement to help improve productivity

Como Plastics

Plastics company improves labor relations and profits using teamwork and owner involvement

ComSonics Incorporated

Inc. 500 growth company combines ESOP and employee participation to meet goals

Continental Insurance Company

Measuring white-collar productivity in a large insurance company proved possible, but modifying standards to meet organizational and technological change proved a greater challenge

Dana Corporation
Diversified vehicular-components manufacturer designs outstanding productivity program based on communications, full disclosure, and participative management

Diamond Fiber Products (formerly Diamond International)
Small-gift club recognizes workers who "do their job well," reducing absenteeism 42 percent and creating employees who feel appreciated

Donnelly Corporation
Midwest auto supplier uses employee ideas to achieve competitive edge

Farmers Home Administration (FmHA)
Computerized resource management system provides quantitative and qualitative measures of field office productivity

Ford Motor Company
U.S. automobile manufacturer finds continual quality improvement the key to customer satisfaction

GE's Daytona Simulation and Control Systems
Robots build simulation and control systems faster and better

GE's Meter and Control Business Department
GE converts old factory to high productivity using computerized materials handling and new addition on the roof

GE's Erie Locomotive Plant
GE refurbishes 70-year-old industrial plant, increasing productivity more than 240 percent

Great Salt Lake Minerals and Chemicals Corporation
Shift schedules in tune with workers' circadian rhythms boost productivity and lessen fatigue in round-the-clock operation

Hewitt Associates
Benefits consulting firm designs program for employees juggling work and parenting responsibilities

Hewlett-Packard Company
Total quality-control program achieves tenfold increase in reliability at major electronics firm

Honeywell Inc.
Participative productivity programs proliferate, producing prodigious profits

Hughes Aircraft Company
Managers learn how to improve personal and company productivity in one-day training session

Humana Inc.
Central computer purchasing system results in savings of $85 million over three-year period

Huron Machine Products, Inc.
Manufacturer implements employee training program to realize maximum yield from FMS investment

Intel Corporation
Earlier productivity techniques became a way of life while new techniques pay off in a "meaner, leaner" organization

Joint Labor Management Committee, Retail Food Industry
Structured cooperation between union and management engenders trust, stability, and foresight

Kitchell Corporation
Comprehensive participative management program helps to develop new managers for future growth

Lincoln Electric Company
Incentive system helps maximize both wages and profits for welding equipment manufacturer

Lowe's Companies, Inc.
Employees in specialty retail chain work for themselves through employee stock ownership plan

McCreary Tire & Rubber Company
Distributing layoffs through furlough rotation helps tire manufacturer cut direct labor costs and shift into new lines of production

Motorola, Inc.
Electronics manufacturer initiates participative management program that gives everyone a chance to improve the business

New United Motor Manufacturing Inc.
UAW joins Japanese management in manufacturing small cars in California; will it work?

New York City Department of Sanitation
Employee participation program transforms New York City bureau into "profit center"

Nucor Corporation
New steel technology results in lower manufacturing costs

Palatine Police Department
Dual-career ladder offers police officers higher earnings for expanded competence and increases departmental productivity

PENNTAP
Costly technical assistance and information available to businesses free

Prince Corporation
Pay-for-performance program helps auto-parts manufacturer evaluate employees more objectively

The Procter & Gamble Company
Job-enlargement plan based on pay-for-skills program and delegation of responsibility creates P&G's most productive plant

Productivity and Responsibility Increase Development and Employment (PRIDE)
Construction industry cooperation succeeds in St. Louis, leads to similar efforts across the United States

The Prudential Insurance Company of America
Job redesign increases employee motivation and results in a 53 percent quality improvement

Shippers' Associations
Shippers' associations pool cargo to reduce freight charges

Softool Corporation
New computer program for data centers and programmers improves the quality of the software they produce and increases productivity

The Travelers Insurance Company
Un-retirement plan provides company with the valuable experience and mature judgment of trained and enthusiastic workers

TRW Inc.
Electronics mail system speeds decision-making process for diversified electronics manufacturer

UAW-Ford National Education Development and Training Program
Joint union/management training program benefits both auto manufacturer and its employees

Westinghouse Electric Corporation
Changing business realities spur nuclear technology division to staff for service, not design

> *The thing that scares me now is that we*
> *know our true costs, but competitors don't.*
> —Richard P. Simmons
> President and CEO

ALLEGHENY LUDLUM
CORPORATION

Computerized cost-measurement system,
aided by nonfunctionalized management
organization, helps achieve 45 percent
productivity improvement

The Program

Allegheny Ludlum makes 126 standard grades of stainless
steel and over 400 varieties. Throw in exotic alloys, and the
number rises to the thousands. All told, the company has
26,000 recipes for making specialty steels, and it changes
1,000 each month. A coil can go through thirty phases of
rolling, annealing, pickling, rerolling, and polishing in two
or three plants before it's finished.

A ton of specialty steel can take five times more worker-
hours to produce than a ton of carbon steel. So companywide managing of costs is a continuing necessity. Five years
of number crunching went into developing a data base
sophisticated enough to model every specialty process.
Today, the system can track every nickel's worth of nickel
from furnace through twelve-ton coil for each of 30,000
coils of steel scheduled around the company's seven plants.

This information system also evaluates every order and schedules its production. Each order is analyzed by size, profit margin, and production allocations, all aimed at assuring profitability and overall efficiency. Then the computer allocates each order's slot in a production run, and tracks the process using bar code tags and readers.

Evaluation

Allegheny Ludlum has managed to string together more than forty consecutive profitable quarters. At 14 percent, its return on total capital is equal to that of any major domestic steel producer, and its debt has been reduced to 35 percent of capital.

Over the last six and a half years, the number of tons produced per worker-hour has increased 45 percent, while in the last four years the quality index has risen 30 percent. Workers at the New Castle, Indiana, plant produce a ton of stainless sheet every four worker-hours—perhaps 50 percent faster than any competing plant. Overall, the company produces over $250,000 in sales per hourly employee.

Productivity improvement at Allegheny Ludlum is largely due to its sophisticated computerized cost-control system, but its success has been aided by management teams organized along six product lines—not by function. Each team is responsible for achieving specified profit targets rather than sales or productivity quotas.

> The employee-owners of America West
> have formed a partnership with
> management in a strong commitment for
> success. As stockholders of the company,
> these highly motivated professionals have a
> spirit of teamwork that results in a quality
> product for the traveling public.
> —Edward R. Beauvais
> Chairman and CEO

AMERICA WEST AIRLINES

New national carrier combines employee
stock ownership, job cross-utilization,
fuel-efficient aircraft, and a hub city
operation to achieve high employee
morale and productivity

The Program

As one of the new low-fare carriers established after dereg-
ulation of the airline industry, Phoenix-based America
West began with a "clean slate" in developing its organizational and productivity programs.

Its plan for success had four central precepts: Establish a
dominant position at Phoenix Sky Harbor International
Airport, utilizing it as a gateway to the West; fly modern,
fuel-efficient aircraft; create high employee productivity
and morale through employee ownership, incentive stock
options, and profit sharing; and offer high-quality service
at low fares.

America West now schedules more than 170 daily departures from Sky Harbor Airport, double the number of its closest competitor. By using its dominant position in Phoenix and Las Vegas, where it operates nearly 100 daily flights, the airline has developed a "superhub" concept, offering modern, uncongested terminals that makes these cities attractive alternatives to the other "gateways" to the West, such as Denver.

The entire America West fleet consists of more than seventy Boeing aircraft, most of them 737s, considered the most fuel-efficient passenger planes in the world. Boeing 757s, 747s, and de Havilland Dash 8s allow the carrier to access both long- and short-distance markets, and make its fleet one of the world's most modern. By the end of 1989, its fleet had become one of *the* most modern.

New America West employees purchase company stock equal to 20 percent of their first year's base salary. The stock is discounted 15 percent from the market value, and a low-rate company financing program is available. An incentive stock option program has also been developed for all employees. And whenever the company produces a profit, employees are rewarded with profit-sharing checks, distributed on a quarterly basis. Profit-sharing amounts are determined by each employee's base salary and seniority in the company, on an annual basis.

Every one of America West's customer service representatives (CSRs) is trained to work a variety of positions. A typical workweek will find a CSR taking reservations, issuing tickets, loading baggage, and operating as a flight attendant. This cross-utilization program increases each CSR's knowledge of the total operation and creates an extremely productive employee.

A number of innovations have also been introduced to increase customer satisfaction. Among the amenities: complimentary cocktails, assigned seating, large overhead storage bins, free copies of *The Wall Street Journal* and *USA Today*, and full interline services. A frequent-flyer program, FlightFUND, rewards those business travelers who do not have the luxury of taking advantage of America

West's lowest fares, which require advance purchase. In addition, the "Careliner" bus service takes passengers to and from Terminal III at Sky Harbor Airport to Scottsdale and Mesa, Arizona, while the "Phoenix Club," a luxurious VIP lounge, offers members the rest and relaxation required for every trip, whether business or pleasure.

Evaluation

America West inaugurated service on August 1, 1983, with three aircraft serving five cities. Today, it is the nation's tenth-largest carrier serving forty-five destinations with more than 10,000 employees. Passenger enplanements are over the 1 million mark for each month, and operating revenues reached almost $800 million in 1988.

> *In today's highly competitive environment,*
> *all companies are looking for some type of*
> *edge. We look for this edge in productivity*
> *improvement.*
> —William Schneider, Director
> Industrial Engineering Group

AMERICAN SEATING COMPANY

Cost-reduction teams use committee
process to set productivity goals and
provide the plans and operating
leadership to achieve them

The Program

The American Seating Company is the world's largest producer of seats (for stadiums, schools, buses, etc.) and a
major manufacturer of office furniture. Its sales exceed
$100 million a year.

For a long period of time, American Seating had used
informal committees in production, engineering, and
other parts of the company to look for ways to improve
productivity. In 1982, however, the president decided to
formalize the process into the Cost Reduction Committee
System, expanding it to all areas of the company (e.g.,
inventory control, returned goods) and making it an integral part of American Seating.

These cost-reduction committees contained four to ten supervisors and managers drawn from different areas of the company, and each committee member was required to attend a training session to become familiar with other departments and to learn techniques that would help him or her make the most of the committee process. Each committee established its own goals for productivity improvement and put a precise monetary value on the savings it hoped to achieve. Once these goals were set, the committee then attempted to accomplish them as it saw fit, purchasing new equipment, for example, or redesigning a production line. Committee chairpersons also met on a regular basis with a steering committee to discuss progress, problems, setbacks, and other matters of mutual concern.

Evaluation

The Cost Reduction Committee System was ended at American Seating in November 1987 and will not be used again. Instead, each functional area in the company has now been made responsible for establishing and meeting its own cost-reduction targets.

The committee system, however, did accomplish three important objectives: (1) It helped save the company money; (2) it cross-trained managers from different departments; and (3) it created a new team spirit by showing employees how to work together on a project.

It also helped bring about significant—and permanent—productivity increases. A robotics committee, for example, had been looking into equipment improvements for some time. So the company purchased a robotic mig welder, which increased productivity over 50 percent in the welding portion of the operation.

As a result of such decisions, the company has realized millions of dollars in savings since 1982, with savings of $3.58 million in 1986 alone, the last year for which specific savings information was provided.

There are two basic motivating opportunities for independent Amway distributors. The first is selling products and services, and the other is an opportunity to develop a sales organization by sponsoring new distributors.
—Amway Corporation Brochure

AMWAY CORPORATION

Dual-opportunity reward system motivates independent sales distributors and helps company achieve $1.9 billion in sales

The Program

All direct-sales organizations face the challenge of how to keep the motivation of their sales force high and commissions equitable. At the Amway Corporation, a sophisticated reward and recognition system does just that, and it has helped Amway's one million distributors worldwide chalk up sales revenues of more than $1.9 billion at suggested retail prices a year.

What is even more surprising is that Amway's entire sales force consists of independent businesspeople who come from all walks of life, not employees of the company. Their income from Amway is based on a commission that averages 30 percent if they sell the company's products at the suggested retail price (though they may, in fact, sell at any price they want) and a performance bonus.

The performance bonus is calculated on the basis of two sets of numbers: Point Value (PV), which does not change, and Business Volume (BV), a dollar value that changes with inflation. At the present time, 1 point of PV is equal to approximately $1.65 BV.* The greater the total PV sold by a distributor, the greater the percentage of bonus paid on Business Volume.

A distributor who sells 100 PV (or $200 BV) in one month, for example, and averages 30 percent in commissions, receives a total income of $66 for that month (30 percent × $200 + 3 percent Performance Bonus on $200).

Amway distributors can also earn additional income by finding and sponsoring other distributors. In fact, the company will pay each distributor a special bonus based on the total sales of all new distributors sponsored. Once a distributor starts sponsoring others, however, it is his or her responsibility to pay their performance bonus. The potential income that can be earned by a sponsoring distributor is calculated in the example opposite.

(Remember, however, that this is only an example. Sponsoring distributors earn more or less based on their monthly performance, and as the table above shows, the performance bonus can reach as high as 25 percent.)

Besides their monetary compensation, Amway distributors are recognized in many other ways. With rising sales volume comes eligibility for awards and designations, and those who truly excel can even win trips and cars. Any time anyone achieves a new sales plateau, his or her picture is also featured in the Amway magazine, the *Amagram*.

Evaluation

Amway's unique compensation, reward, and recognition system has helped total company sales grow from $500,000 in 1959 to $1.9 billion at suggested retail prices today. And it is flexible enough to allow the company to focus on dif-

---

* Note: For purposes of illustration, the round figure of $2.00 is used in the example.

Monthly PV	Performance Bonus
100	3% of BV (Business Volume)
300	6%
600	9%
1,000	12%
1,500	15%
2,500	18%
4,000	21%
6,000	23%
7,500	25%

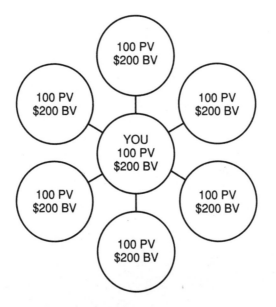

Total Monthly PV 700
Total Monthly BV $1,400

9% Performance Bonus	
($1,400 × 9%)	$ 126
You Pay	− $ 36
You Keep	$ 90
30% Basic Discount (on $200)	+ $ 60
Monthly Gross Income	$ 150
Annualized Gross Income	$1,800

ferent business objectives as conditions in the marketplace change. At the present time, for example, the company is introducing a number of new product lines and promotion programs to emphasize the many ways current Amway distributors can increase their income. The result is that in recent years the company's sales per distributor have increased dramatically. These enhanced sales opportunities also provide an additional incentive for any would-be distributors who wish to own and operate a business of their own.

> *We can make a Mac every twenty seconds.*
> —Apple Management

APPLE COMPUTER, INC.

Just-in-time inventory control and materials flow systems provide improved quality, increased productivity, and lower cost in high-tech manufacturing plant

The Program

Since November 1983, Apple's MacIntosh computer plant has manufactured over 2 million machines. One reason for this enormous productivity is the fact that the MacIntosh factory has implemented a just-in-time inventory system to control materials flow. Before parts are distributed to their production locations, they are categorized and recorded in the factory's computer control system, and all purchased materials are tested for quality as they enter the plant.

Each part is classified into one of two categories: bulk parts and small parts. Bulk parts include video displays, chassis, housings, and power supplies; small parts are items like integrated circuits and microprocessors. Bulk materials are distributed to the proper work stations by an overhead parts-delivery system, while automated storage and retrieval systems handle the small parts, distributing them to the work centers where they are needed. If workers need more parts, they can put their empty part-totes on a conveyor that automatically sends them back for refills.

Other parts are carried to work stations by robot-like automated vehicles that are battery-powered and can freely maneuver around the factory floor. Workers can request parts from the robotic system from their work station terminals.

Evaluation

Apple's materials-flow system has reduced inventory costs while maintaining a steady flow of parts into the work areas where they are needed. Compared to a manual assembly line, this automated system has achieved a remarkable number of efficiencies, including:

1. A 53 percent direct labor saving
2. A 17 percent overhead saving
3. A 20 percent total cost saving

Today, Apple is automating even further to improve its production process. But when we asked about the newest improvements that have been made, the company's managers would respond only with a sales pitch for their newest Mac, a clear affirmation of the old rule: *sine emptor nullum negotium*—without a customer, you are out of business. This combination of the traditional free-enterprise ethic and cutting-edge technological improvements makes Apple one of the better competitors in what is perhaps our most competitive field.

> *Quality will determine who wins in the
> competitive banking market.*
> —William Latzko
> Consultant

THE BANK OF NEW YORK

Bank's statistical quality-control
procedures lower error rates by as much
as 70 percent

The Program

In banking, quality is measured by the way in which services are delivered to the bank's customers. But each day, a bank performs tens of thousands of clerical tasks, and thousands of errors are made. The need to correct these errors before they reach the customer led The Bank of New York to develop a statistical quality-control approach to "tame the paper tiger" called QUIP (Quality Improvement Program).

QUIP helps improve production quality in the bank's clerical systems by measuring the four "costs" that each system has to manage:

1. *Appraisal Cost*—the cost of checking or verifying that the work has been done correctly

2. *Internal Failure Cost*—the cost of wasted effort and any rework

3. *External Failure Cost*—the cost incurred by the next system as a result of receiving incorrect input

4. *Prevention Cost*—the cost of quality-control efforts

By focusing specifically on reducing internal failure costs, managers who use QUIP have found that they can significantly reduce all the other costs.

Supervisors who have been trained in QUIP sample the output of each of their clerks regularly and keep an ongoing record of the quality of the work being produced. If an error is discovered during sampling, a supervisor attempts to "fix the problem, not the blame." Then, using these individual output files and statistical analysis, the supervisor can determine the precise capability of each clerical system. Comparing individual output to these standards helps supervisors focus on those areas of individual performance that need improvement.

Evaluation

In general, the QUIP system has resulted in a drastic reduction in internal failure at The Bank of New York, eliminating 50 to 70 percent of the mistakes that had previously been made. There has also been a definite impact on external failure rates. By reducing the number of mistakes made in the first place, fewer mistakes are reaching the customer. This has resulted in substantial savings in out-of-pocket expenses and has improved customer relations. The latter, while intangible, can nevertheless be quite real, especially when quality is improving to such an extent that senior management is receiving direct feedback on it from customers. The bank is now working on a new strategy that can better measure how the quality of its work is living up to customer expectations.

> *BEA is seeking to diminish the separation of "decision" and "execution" to counter the tendency to fragment work typical of larger firms.*
>
> —Corporate Philosophy

BEA ASSOCIATES, INC.

Fund management firm retains key money managers and achieves spectacular growth through participative compensation and centralized operational support

The Program

Participative management was adopted at BEA to promote individual achievement and provide the effective collaboration necessary for implementing investment strategies.

Eight asset fund managers are the company's core managing group. Assisted by one backup manager, each is responsible for his or her client's investments. Performance is measured monthly by the return on investment of the funds under management, adjusted for risk and diversification, with the results reviewed by the other fund managers.

Each year, BEA's fund management performance is analyzed by a research unit that determines where value was added and by whom. Then all eight fund managers study the report and indicate in writing what they think their own and their associates' compensation should be. These votes are collected and read aloud (only the vote results are made public), and a simple average of the votes is used to determine a fund manager's total compensation. The system eliminates politicking, encourages communication among peers, allocates rewards where achievement is clear, and publicly reinforces desired performance.

To avoid growing "islands" of staff around each fund manager, operational and clerical support units have been centralized. Headed by only one administrator, these units provide support for all eight fund managers.

Evaluation

Investment management is a business noted for independent thinkers and high turnover. But in thirteen years, BEA has lost only three money managers. The assets it manages have grown about 30 percent annually, from $100 million to $6 billion, even though the number of its employees has increased just 67 percent, a payroll increase that represents only 3 percent of the company's growth in discretionary assets.

BEA's integrated approach to participative management may prove to be useful in other companies where talented individuals require close collaboration to achieve superior results.

> *Everyone's looking for an edge these days: something to improve margins, raise product quality, or keep employees interested in their jobs. Many Beatrice companies have found that edge—through productivity improvement.*
> —Beatrice Productivity Guidebook

BEATRICE COMPANIES, INC.

Giant manufacturer installs total productivity program at 150 profit centers and achieves $50 million in savings

The Program

When Beatrice Companies decided to institute a five-step productivity improvement program in 1979, Step 1 was to create a basic awareness through the company of the need to improve productivity. This was accomplished largely by including productivity presentations at management meetings, by contributing articles on productivity to employee newsletters, and by developing special audiovisual materials for use in employee gatherings. The company's chairman of the board also sent a letter to each division president emphasizing the message that Beatrice was serious about improving its overall productivity.

Step 2 in the program was employee education. This was accomplished through a series of two-and-a-half-day Productivity Improvement Workshops directed toward profit center presidents, directors of manufacturing, and productivity coordinators. The workshops focused on four major areas:

- Managing for productivity improvement
- Involving employees
- Developing tools, techniques, and case studies on productivity improvement
- Developing specific action plans

Step 3, recognizing employee achievement, placed great importance on creating the proper incentives for change. This was accomplished through a subsidiary program called Uncommon People, Uncommon Goals, which allowed each profit center to decide where it would like to focus its productivity efforts, what goals it would set, and what kinds of awards it would give out:

> Each time goals are met, you'll be eligible for awards. The exact type of award will be decided by your company. Typical awards range from free coffee and rolls every day for a period of time to company-sponsored special events for employees and their spouses—like a concert or a ball game.*

Beatrice also developed its Star Award for those managers whose units recorded exceptional improvements in productivity. Hung in the manager's office for all to see, the Star Award was the company's "biggest sales tool in selling productivity," according to manager of productivity improvement Mike Bremer.

Measuring the results of the program in actual dollars saved was Step 4 of the productivity improvement effort, while Step 5 was integrating productivity into the company's overall business plan. "For the program to sustain itself, productivity goals had to tie into the company's profit goals," says Bremer. And this was done chiefly at the local level, where each profit center was allowed to identify its

---

* Beatrice Productivity Guidebook.

own productivity objectives, establish the programs it needed to meet them, and calculate its expected results.

Evaluation

Beatrice's five-step productivity improvement program produced impressive results, especially between the years 1981 and 1985.

Year	Profit Centers Participating	Savings
FY 81	13	$ 7,000,000
FY 82	140	$27,000,000
FY 83	150	$40,000,000
FY 84	N.A.	$50,000,000

At Beatrice, productivity improvement is not an option, it is a necessity. And management knows that the key to any successful improvement effort is the people who make it happen and succeed.

Ted E. Olson, previously a Beatrice operations vice-president, reports that Beatrice management recognized that employees were the key to success in becoming more competitive:

Motivated employees mean better productivity. Better productivity means more jobs, higher demand for products made, increased sales, greater profits, and, therefore higher pay and better benefits for all.

Note: Beatrice Companies, Inc. was purchased in April 1986 by BCI Holdings Corporation in a leveraged buyout. The company has since reorganized under a new management team.

Especially when money market funds were new and we had a lot of explaining to do, a computerized phone service's help was enormous.

—Wayne Sibly
Former Chairman and CEO

CALVERT GROUP

Computerized telephone system creates satisfied customers for financial services organization

The Program

When the Calvert Group started offering a popular new money market mutual fund to investors, the company soon found that the traditional telephone system it was working with was woefully inadequate to meet its growing business needs. Reaching the company was frustrating and difficult for customers, and the morale of employees was being adversely affected by the constant barrage of complaints they were hearing.

After carefully evaluating all the new technologies available, the company decided to purchase a Rolm MCBX with automatic call distribution. The MCBX balances the work load of telephone representatives by automatically apportioning incoming calls based on the number of calls waiting, the length of time they have been on hold, and the average length of time each call takes to answer. The system can also be programmed to divert incoming calls to "flex team" employees during peak periods, thereby decreasing waiting time and increasing customer service. The hard data collected by the system over time can also be used to determine staffing needs.

Evaluation

The Calvert Group was so pleased with the performance of its Rolm MCBX that the company decided to upgrade the system to incorporate "voice response." This technology allows a customer to indicate what kind of service or information he or she needs without talking to a Calvert employee. Merely by pushing a button on a touch-tone phone, a customer can place an order, check an account balance, or find out the daily yield on a money market mutual fund.

For management at the Calvert Group, there is no question that the use of a computerized telephone system has increased the number of satisfied customers and improved employee morale as well. Staff members no longer have to spend time handling routine inquiries, and can devote themselves fully to addressing the more substantive concerns of their clients. The system has allowed the company to accommodate a substantial increase in customers without having to hire additional staff and, as an unexpected benefit, the company has also been able to reduce its overall telephone costs.

> *It is an historic breakthrough, not only in labor-management relations, but also in meeting the national need to improve productivity.*
>
> —*Los Angeles Times*

CERTIFIED GROCERS OF CALIFORNIA LTD.

Labor/management plan rewards more productive warehouse workers with time off and extra pay

The Program

At the outset, Certified Grocers sought to increase productivity and profits in its multibillion-dollar wholesale grocery business by targeting three specific areas: (1) warehouse operations, (2) accounting, and (3) data processing. Quality circles were formed in all three areas and their efforts were coordinated with a steering group chaired by company senior vice-president Don Gross who met regularly with a broad spectrum of employees. A standing committee that included truck drivers and traffic superintendents was also set up in the transportation department.

The warehouse quality circle was the first to come up with a workable suggestion for productivity in its area. It recommended that an incentive system be established in which certain rewards—either extra pay or time off with pay—be granted to those workers whose performance exceeded the average work performance or an agreed-upon standard.

Local Teamsters Union 595 played an important part in setting the warehouse work standards. It brought in a team of experts to work with the company's production engineers in determining a fair standard against which actual work performance could be measured and bonuses paid. Senior vice-president for distribution Bob Walz also agreed that certified employees would be strongly motivated by the opportunity to earn paid leisure time, so he decided to make paid time off a key reward in the program and worked together with both top management and the rank and file to develop acceptance performance criteria and an attractive reward schedule.

The performance standards that were eventually accepted are based on engineer evaluations of how much work can be accomplished by an average worker within the existing work environment. Past performance achievements played a role in devising these performance standards, but it should be noted that they are *not* historical averages that are raised whenever the company's overall productivity takes a leap. This avoids penalizing steady workers who, for whatever reason, are unwilling or unable to increase their productivity.

This is how the system works: Every employee earns .45 minute of paid time off for every hour of work performed that measures between 100.5 and 114 percent of the engineering-based standard. If the employee produces at a level exceeding 114 percent of the standard, he or she receives .60 minute per hour for every percentage point above 100.5.

That means that an employee who works thirty-five hours at 115 percent of standard earns 304.5 minutes (35 × .60 minutes × [115− 100.5]) of time off with pay. This time off can be accumulated for one quarter but must be used up during the following quarter. If the employee desires, he or she can choose a financial reward instead that is equal to one-half the time pay for the earned time off.

The system set up at Certified works in such a way that

efficient and productive workers are rewarded, but slow workers are not penalized as long as they stay within 10 percent of standard. If a worker drops below 90 percent of standard, however, Certified does apply disciplinary measures that include verbal and written warnings, and temporary and permanent dismissal. But there are also features to the system that allow an employee to remove these "black marks" permanently from his or her record.

Evaluation

During the first year it was installed at Certified, the new incentive program helped the company increase productivity more than 15 percent and save more than $2 million in payroll costs. And these savings have increased every year since then. The company has been able to encourage above-average performance without paying overtime, hiring more workers, or paying more fringe benefits for the extra work done. In addition to that, it has experienced a dramatic decrease in absenteeism, employee turnover, and labor grievances.

The program is simple and basic and can be replicated almost anywhere there is a measurable production standard. Other food retailers, such as Ralph's, Von's, and Safeway, have implemented similar programs. It is the kind of incentive system that has all the ingredients for success: It has the support of labor and management, it offers rewards that motivate people, and it is fair.

> *The goal of creating a corporate identity*
> *was to develop closer ties between the*
> *company and its employees.*
> —Aubrey Cole
> Senior Vice-Prsident

CHAMPION INTERNATIONAL

$4 billion conglomerate develops corporate philosophy of employee involvement to help improve productivity

The Program

Each of the formerly independent companies that merged to create Champion International had its own corporate identity, but Champion had no image that employees could relate to. This lack of identity did not create a sound environment for productivity improvement, thought CEO Andrew C. Sigler, so he decided to develop a corporate philosophy called the Champion Way. In addition, Sigler decided to ask employees for their suggestions on how to cut costs and improve productivity at Champion's paper-pulp and wood operations.

As envisioned by Sigler, the Champion Way is a seven-step approach to creating a new corporate culture. It includes:

1. *The Champion Way Statement*—an outline of the goals and objectives of the company that clearly tells everyone where everyone else is headed.

2. *Communication*—the use of an Involvement Team Approach to create broad, open lines of communication. These teams, which are strictly voluntary and self-organized, look for production problems in their work areas and attempt to eliminate them. "Any financial savings achieved by the team are a side benefit," says senior vice-president Aubrey Cole. "The main idea is involvement." The company is also running a series of ads nationwide, more for the purpose of achieving a unified corporate identity than for any marketing reasons.

3. *Training and Development*—a set of comprehensive programs for managers and future managers. One program, Managing for Excellence, is a "fast-track" course for middle managers with high potential that focuses on financial and human resources training. Several other specialized programs are also available for foremen who want to improve the way they supervise front-line workers.

4. *Work Environment Tangibles*—a commitment to improving working conditions in Champion's plants and offices.

5. *Work Environment Intangibles*—ways to build trust between labor and management. Since the company's union was slow to embrace the Champion Way, management works hard to keep the union well informed of what it is doing and why as a means of building confidence.

6. *Organizational Structures*—attempts to structure the organization of company businesses in a manner consistent with both product and people.

7. *Employee and Community Activities*—full support to those who involve themselves in extracurricular activities either at the company or in their community.

The Involvement Team Approach has been used primarily to address production problems at Champion's paper-pulp and wood operations. When a specific problem is identified in any area of the mill, the area supervisor begins recruiting a team by identifying eight to ten interested lower-level managers and line employees. Normally, the first-line supervisor serves as team leader, but company coordinators and facilitators are also used to explain the benefits of team participation and lead the newly assembled team through problem-identification techniques.

Once operational, a team meets at least once a month to discuss the nature and cause of the problem and to identify possible solutions. When the team has reached a consensus, its solution is presented to the area supervisor, who must decide whether or not to implement it. If the supervisor's response is positive, the team has the option of staying together to work on other problems.

Evaluation

As a result of the Champion Way, employee morale at Champion International seems to be higher and the team concept is spreading quickly throughout the organization. In the first three years, twenty-three teams were formed in the paper-pulp division, saving the company $1 million at the Pasadena mill alone. The company estimates that the teams helped save $4 million in the entire paper division the first year they were set up.

COMO PLASTICS

Plastics company improves labor
relations and profits using teamwork and
owner involvement

The Program

Como Plastics, a maker of molded plastic framing used
by manufacturers of high-technology equipment, had a
history of poor labor relations during the 1970s; strikes in
both 1973 and 1976 reflected the turmoil. So when C. W.
Jackson purchased the company in 1980, he decided to
approach management matters differently. He installed a
new management team and imposed a new management
philosophy: teamwork.

By 1988, the philosophy of employee involvement had
become a way of life, as had Total Quality Control and the
just-in-time production system. Management now takes an
active position in being not only the leader but also the
disciple of the employee involvement religion. Words like
"survival" are included in every expression of the company's philosophy and management style and the active ap-

proach highlights "cost management" rather than "cost accounting."

How did Como do it?

1. At the outset, specific goals were established and articulated:

a. Plant utilization would be raised to 80 percent (even though the industry average was only 72 percent).

b. Pre-tax profit margins would be raised to 8 percent (the industry average was 6 percent), and a system for paying bonuses based on achieving profit targets would be established.

2. Personalized labor/management relations were made a necessary ingredient in any effort to move the company ahead. It started with the first-ever company Christmas party with gifts and entertainment. Then an annual picnic was made a company tradition, as were Thanksgiving turkeys and Christmas hams. Eventually it became apparent to everyone that the company's management did view its work force as consisting of real people.

3. Sharing information was made a key step in motivating employees and getting their views on important company matters. Once a month now, a member of management meets with all staff personnel to discuss the company's production problems and financial performance during the previous month. Twice a month a member of management meets with twenty members of the production staff where the same information is released, but in a more condensed form. According to the president, these regular meetings make everyone "feel more a part of the whole thing."

In addition, the chairman and the president have breakfast with twelve or thirteen employees on a monthly basis, where anything is open for discussion—from production techniques and profits to new product lines and retirement benefits. The company also encourages the formation of quality circles and has a record of implementing about 75–80 percent of all circle recommendations.

Evaluation

After Como Plastics changed hands and employee involvement was made an integral part of the corporate culture, sales volume more than doubled, from $8 million in 1980 to $17 million in 1983, while profits increased 800 percent in the same period. In addition, a new union contract that both sides felt was equitable and fair was signed in 1986 after only three days of negotiations and four meetings. Labor grievances, which had reached up to thirty-five a year before 1980, were totally eliminated.

Today, labor/management relations at Como Plastics are generally excellent, and the teamwork environment permits previously unthinkable goals to become a reality. Employees have truly become part of the company team and they know it.

> *It has always been my firm belief that employees contribute to the growth of a company as much as capital, and employees should, therefore, participate in that growth.*
>
> —Warren L. Braun
> Chairman and CEO

COMSONICS INCORPORATED

Inc. 500 growth company combines ESOP and employee participation to meet goals

The Program

When Warren Braun started ComSonics in 1972, it was his idea that all employees should share in the responsibility of running the company as well as in reaping the financial rewards from it. He chose two methods to achieve his goal: participatory management and employee ownership.

His first step was to provide a vehicle that would help employees share in the company's success—an employee stock ownership plan (ESOP). But "after the first year," says Braun, "I found myself with a disaster on my hands. It was as if the employees had been handed a stone rather than the tools to work for greater profits." One of the reasons the ESOP was failing was that employees did not understand what an ESOP was or how it worked to their benefit.

To overcome this obstacle, the company undertook a

massive educational program to instruct everyone in the basics of stock ownership, stock value, and the part employees can play in improving that value.

Working in tandem with the ESOP program is a participatory management system based on the principle of "operation by objective." Each company, division, and employee at ComSonics is given a set of goals and may attempt to achieve them in whatever way that is deemed best. Today, strategic planning is done not only at the top levels of the company, but also in the middle and at the bottom. "Such a system takes flexibility by the chief executive officer," says Braun. "They will make some mistakes, and at times you just want to dump the whole thing."

To provide a forum for the exchange of ideas, managers and supervisors each hold two meetings a month. The first deals with operational issues—analyzing the current budget, where the company stands in making the budget, the upcoming budget, and what improvements and gains have been made and can be made. The second meeting involves longer-range planning—looking at goals, projections, and expectations.

Then, once a month, there is a "free-for-all" meeting where supervisors and managers leave their titles outside the door; anything is open for discussion. "When these meetings first began," says Braun, "there was a lot of finger pointing. But today everybody is more concerned with the company's goals and objectives and how they can best be met." It is important to note that all these meetings take place with the chief executive officer *not* in attendance, helping to make sure their discussions remain free and uninhibited.

In 1986–1987, the company bolstered its commitment to worker participation by setting up an Employee Advisory Committee and allowing direct employee voting in board meetings. As a result, any thinking about policy decisions and the setting of goals does not stop at the supervisory level but continues down throughout the company. Because all employees are stockholders, even production workers are considered one of the four levels of manage-

ment and are expected to help in the decision-making process.

Evaluation

In 1987, overall corporate profits at ComSonics increased
by 300 percent. Over the past five years, the company has
been on *Inc.* magazine's list of the 500 fastest-growing companies in America, its sales volume increasing during the
period more than 260 percent.

ComSonics continues to grow at an accelerated rate.
From 1985 through 1989 the stock price nearly doubled,
from $5.00 to $9.80 per share. The company also was
awarded the U.S. Senate Bronze Medal for Productivity.

I should have been more aggressive. If I had known what we would save through this program, I would have been willing to spend more money on it earlier.

—John Bretherick
President

CONTINENTAL INSURANCE COMPANY

Measuring white-collar productivity in a large insurance company proved possible, but modifying standards to meet organizational and technological change proved a greater challenge

The Program

Continental Insurance operated its domestic property and casualty business through forty branch offices throughout the United states, and various analyses had shown that branch expenses were ranging from 3 percent to 13 percent of total premium income. In an effort to control and standardize these branch expenses, the company developed a Productivity Performance Index (PPI) using existing branch office data.

Three different measurements are totaled to calculate a branch office's PPI. First, to evaluate staffing levels and compare branch office efficiencies, a Productivity Indicator weights transaction costs according to difficulty for each processing unit in the branch. Second, the ratio of transactions expenses to premium income is calculated to evaluate relative costs of processing. Finally, service timeliness is measured by figuring the average number of days required to process different insurance instruments. When added together, these measurements produce the PPI: an accurate indicator of a branch office's productivity, expenses, and effectiveness that can be calculated merely by compiling data that are routinely forwarded to the company's main office.

Using the PPI, the company's Productivity Research and Development Department had produced a 200-page manual of procedures, called the *Branch Office Productivity Guide*, that had been used to bring about significant technological and organizational changes within the company. New standards to meet new procedures are currently being developed, with implementation expected in little more than a year, and the measurements that result from these changes will be incorporated in a new productivity enhancement program.

Evaluation

In its first year of using the PPI, Continental increased its productivity (work load compared to staffing) by 18.4 percent, raised its service levels by 12.5 percent, and reduced its branch expenses by 5 percent. Relying only on attrition and early retirement, its total branch office staff fell 20 percent. By 1986, however, new sales techniques and office procedures had to be introduced to deal with dramatic changes in the marketplace, so old standards had to be put on hold while new ones were developed. But the company believes that a new PPI standard can be developed, and that it will continue to help in generating additional productivity improvements.

As Continental Insurance has shown, the creative transformation of data into meaningful measures of white-collar productivity is a difficult area to work in, yet it is one of the primary areas of opportunity for achieving productivity improvement today in a growing service-based economy.

> *The only dumb question is the one you do not ask.*
>
> —Dana Folk Saying

DANA CORPORATION

Diversified vehicular-components manufacturer designs outstanding productivity program based on communications, full disclosure, and participative management

The Program

Communication is a key aspect of the total productivity environment at Dana Corporation.

Every employee is scheduled to meet with a senior manager at least once a year, and each Dana facility displays posters with tear-off sheets that are prestamped and pre-addressed to the chairman of the board. Employees are encouraged to write to the chairman if they have a question, a problem, or just want information. Once a quarter, the chairman sends a letter to every employee's home outlining his personal views on the company's future, its market share, and other issues.

During the last seven working days of each month, operating results for every unit and division within Dana are made available, and employees also receive information monthly on the corporation's overall performance and how it compares to the previous year. There is even an 800 number shareholders and employees can call for current information on the company, and questions or suggestions may be left at the end of the taped telephone message.

With no more than five levels of management and a management-by-walking-around style, face-to-face communication has largely replaced memo writing. Extensive job rotation also helps build internal people networks, while promotion from within provides additional incentives for growth. To further promote participation, even budgets are prepared from the bottom up, and all production procedures are developed by those who will actually use them.

Gainsharing plans are used in approximately thirty-five of Dana's manufacturing plants and distribution centers. Whenever productivity increases are registered in a particular plant or center, each person there receives a cash bonus.

Much of Dana's innovative management style has been summed up in what are called the "forty thoughts":

Forty Thoughts

1. Remember our purpose—to earn money for our shareholders and increase the value of their investment.
2. Recognize people as our most important asset.
3. Help people grow.
4. Promote from within.
5. Remember—people respond to recognition.
6. Share the rewards.
7. Provide stability of income and employment.
8. Decentralize.
9. Provide autonomy.
10. Encourage entrepreneurship.
11. Use corporate committees, task forces.
12. Push responsibility down.
13. Involve everyone.
14. Make every employee a manager.
15. Control only what's important.
16. Promote identity with Dana.
17. Make all Dana people shareholders.
18. Simplify.
19. Use little paper.
20. Keep no files.

21. Communicate fully.
22. Let Dana people know first.
23. Let people set goals and judge their performance.
24. Let people decide, where possible.
25. Discourage conformity.
26. Be professional.
27. Break organizational barriers.
28. Develop pride.
29. Insist on high ethical standards.
30. Focus on markets.
31. Utilize assets fully.
32. Contain investment —buy, don't make.
33. Balance plants, products, markets.
34. Keep facilities under 500 people.
35. Stabilize production.
36. Develop proprietary products.
37. Anticipate market needs.
38. Control cash.
39. Deliver reliably.
40. Do what's best for all of Dana.

Evaluation

Dana is now one of the most successful manufacturing companies in the country. Its constant dollar sales per employee have doubled over the last decade, in part because increasing profits through productivity planning has been made an integral part of its corporate culture.

The one word that will have a great impact
on labor/management relations and on how
productivity responds: recognition!
—Daniel C. Boyle
Vice-President and Treasurer

DIAMOND FIBER PRODUCTS (formerly Diamond International)

Small-gift club recognizes workers who "do their job well," reducing absenteeism 42 percent and creating employees who feel appreciated

The Program

Diamond International created the "100 club" at its egg-carton plant as a way of recognizing employees for their contribution to the company.

The idea that the company needed a formal recognition and reward system came about after a grievance committee meeting between the union and management. Daniel C. Boyle, then personnel manager, realized that nothing was being done for the majority of employees who simply did their jobs well. "They don't get the ego massage they need," Boyle pointed out, and his perception was confirmed by an employee survey conducted in 1980. The results of the survey revealed that:

- 65 percent of all employees felt they were not treated respectfully
- 79 percent felt they were not rewarded for a job well done

In addition, employee grievances had risen to 150 a year and work days lost to absenteeism had increased to 3,303.

To rectify the matter, Boyle created the 100 Club in February 1981. The Club rewards employees with points for doing their job well. Points are awarded on an objective basis (e.g., 25 points for 100 percent attendance), and when an employee accumulates 100 points, he or she formally becomes a member of the 100 Club, receiving a blue nylon jacket with a patch signifying membership. Any points earned over 100 can be used to purchase gifts. "The gifts earned with points are not particularly expensive," says Boyle, " and are well within the workers' purchasing power. But the basic premise of the 100 Club is not to 'buy' increased profits and productivity with lavish gifts but to demonstrate management's interest and concern for its employees."

Evaluation

To measure the long-term impact of the program, Diamond International conducted another employee survey in 1983. Its results revealed that:

- 86 percent felt management considered employees to be either "important" or "very important"
- 77 percent felt they were adequately rewarded through "recognition" from their supervisors

At the same time, it was calculated that worker output had increased 16.5 percent, absenteeism had declined 42 percent (with savings of $114,462 in 1982), and worker grievances had dropped to about forty a year.

As a result of these findings, Diamond International decided to install the 100 Club in three of its other plants.

Though installation took about ten weeks and start-up costs totaled nearly $100,000 in the following eighteen months, the company ended up saving over $5 million and experienced a 14.5 percent increase in productivity.

In the past few years, Daniel C. Boyle & Associates, Inc., has begun approximately sixty similar programs around the nation in all types of firms, from manufacturing to service organizations, and at the present time all programs are on or ahead of schedule. Boyle and his partner, Robert E. Arnold, bought the company in 1984. The 100 Club continues to generate productivity growth of about 2.3 percent a year with corresponding improvements in attendance and industrial safety. And many of the same results have been duplicated at other businesses where the 100 Club has been installed, such as Owens-Corning Fiberglas Corporation, Marcus Printing Co., Schulz Electric Co., Nestle Foods Corp., and Heekin Can, Inc.

The 100 Club has been shown to be an effective tool in improving labor/management relations, worker morale, and organizational productivity. It has also proved, according to Boyle, that "the American worker, by way of the Diamond worker as an example, is second to none."

> *Involved Donnelly employees achieve*
> *success. The Donnelly Ideas program is*
> *alive and well—this program was critical to*
> *our success.*
>
> —Dwane Baumgardner
> President

DONNELLY CORPORATION

Midwest auto supplier uses employee
ideas to achieve competitive edge

The Program

The Donnelly Management System, which has taken thirty
years to evolve, does not lend itself well to being picked
apart in piecemeal fashion. Yet even though all its parts
are integrally related to one another, that does not mean
other companies cannot draw valuable ideas from it.

The Donnelly system is based on four basic principles:

1. An organization must build structures and processes
so that employees have the opportunity to participate in
ways that make them feel valued as individuals.

2. The system must be based on competence.

3. The customer must be the focus in all planning and
problem solving.

4. Productivity must be consistently rewarded.

Donnelly uses a modified Scanlon reward system for productivity improvements. A Scanlon plan is a system of re-

warding workers for achieving savings in labor costs. Though many Scanlon plans focus primarily on suggestions, cost reductions, and bonuses, Donnelly also looks for ways to further promote employee participation. It does this primarily through work teams, equity teams, and the Donnelly committee.

Work Teams. The cornerstone of the Donnelly Management System, work teams are groups of employees who report to one boss and have a common mission. Everyone in the organization belongs to at least one work team—including the company president.

Supervisors are the "linchpins" of the work team approach. Their membership on both subordinate teams and peer-level teams allows for information to flow freely up and down the organization. Work teams also have overlapping responsibilities, and try to concern themselves not just with their own objectives, but with the goals and accomplishments of the entire organization.

Equity Committees. There are five equity committees in the corporation, whose members consist of one representative from each work team, each member serving a two-year term. Equity committees deal with personnel policies, wage levels, grievances, and other similar matters, and all their decisions must be reached by unanimous vote. If a decision affects only one area in the company, the committee has the authority to implement it, but if the decision affects more than one area, it must be passed on to the Donnelly Committee.

Donnelly Committee. Made up of fifteen voting members —thirteen from the equity committees, one representative from production supervision, and the president—the Donnelly Committee includes four resource members who do not have voting privileges. As in the equity committees, all decisions made by the Donnelly Committee must be unanimous.

Evaluation

While scores of suppliers to the auto industry are declaring bankruptcy, Donnelly has garnered a bigger share of the market, introduced new products, and increased sales substantially. And this increase in sales has not been limited just to domestic markets. Donnelly now supplies one-third of the mirrors that grace all cars imported from Japan.

Bigger company profits also mean employee payouts at Donnelly, and profit-sharing bonuses in the last few years have averaged 8 percent.

Several years ago, a Ph.D. candidate spent some time at Donnelly to determine whether or not the company really does benefit from its unusual management approach. Taking into consideration all the company's organizational development costs—staff salaries, meeting time, program expenses, training, etc.—he credited half the company's productivity improvements to the Donnelly Management System. He calculated that over a seven-year period, the company's return on investment was 220 percent.

> *The concept and techniques used in this project can be applied to a great many case-processing operations.*
>
> —Donald Kull
> Consultant

FARMERS HOME ADMINISTRATION (FmHA)

Computerized resource management system provides quantitative and qualitative measures of field office productivity

The Program

The Farmers Home Administration is one of the largest lending institutions in the United States and is a vital financial link in rural America. Its 1,910 county offices and 266 district offices make farm, housing, community, and multi-family developer loans. Keeping track of the complex and geographically dispersed FmHA programs is an extraordinary task and one for which a Resource Management System (RMS) was developed.

The RMS identifies the amount of work accomplished at each office as well as the resources required to do it well. Normalized comparisons of time spent performing standard tasks provide a quick measure of the productivity of each FmHA office. Formulation of budgets, projection of staffing requirements, allocation of staff to field offices, classification and grading of personnel positions, identification of work-improvement techniques, monthly management reports, and satisfying Washington-generated ad hoc reports are made possible by the RMS.

Essential to the RMS are the work measurement standards, reviewed annually by outside consultants, which were derived by first analyzing the work performed in individual field offices. A work breakdown structure divides work into individual programs, such as rural housing, farm ownership, and so on, which are further subdivided into reportable accomplishments, such as applications received, appraisals made, loans processed, inspections performed, and delinquent accounts serviced. Each accomplishment is also divided into discrete work steps or work elements. All standards are approved by a representative committee drawn from all major programs in the national office.

Analysis of each work step identifies a time and a frequency for performing the work. Time defines in minutes how long it takes to do a work step once. Frequency defines how many times that work step is done when the field office is credited with performing the reportable accomplishment. Time and frequency data are gathered by a combination of work sampling, auditing records, interviewing field personnel, and analyzing questionnaires.

Evaluation

FmHA uses its RMS to determine its resource needs and in submitting its annual budget requests. The RMS permits it to respond quickly to budget requests. Its value also was demonstrated when FmHA was able to respond quickly in 1988 to a Presidential Executive Order under which it established its Productivity Improvement Program. FmHA efforts in this regard have led to further improvements in quality, timeliness, and efficiency.

FmHA is converting from manual reporting to automated data gathering to make reporting of work accomplished easier. Not only will this improve efficiency, but it

also will ensure that field offices are given full credit for the
work they do.

> *Our focus has shifted from defect detection*
> *to defect prevention and a drive to satisfy*
> *the customer.*
>
> —John Manoogian
> General Manager

FORD MOTOR COMPANY

U.S. automobile manufacturer finds
continual quality improvement the key
to customer satisfaction

The Program

Like it or not, many American auto manufacturers in the
1970s were losing their reputation for competitive quality in
products and services. The reason was that companies like
Ford traditionally relied upon a "reactive" quality-control
system, where the emphasis was on finding and fixing quality problems as quickly as possible rather than on seeking
ways to prevent them. Defects and breakdowns, even if
fixed expeditiously, were costly and inefficient and were no
longer acceptable to the American consumer.

As foreign competition continued to intensify, it became
increasingly more obvious that the find-and-fix approach
had to be replaced. Ford was finding it more difficult to
market cars against higher-quality foreign imports, and was
spending more and more resources to redo what should
have been done right the first time.

The company established a quality-assurance office
charged with the task of putting high quality back into

Ford's products. The first priority was to confirm and publicize the CEO's support for the effort. "Unless you receive the support of the CEO and the president," says then executive director of product assurance John Manoogian, "believe me, you're not going to get to first base."

Under the direction of the new quality-assurance office, the company provided training for all managers that focused on finding opportunities for improving quality in production, and a 171-point checklist was introduced at each assembly plant to pinpoint problems that needed corrective action.

All employees began using the pilot Escort program, which organized workers into reliability teams, where they were trained to understand how quality control helps build a better car. A separate employee involvement program was also used to complement the Quality Is Job One (Q1) effort.

Design and assembly engineers were trained to work together to use statistical process control techniques to measure production variances. Since quality costs can increase as product characteristics vary, Ford invested heavily in advanced technologies like CAD/CAM (computer-aided design/computer-aided manufacturing), flexible manufacturing systems, and automation to reduce product variability and the probability of error.

The Q1 program was also established to recognize suppliers who maintain high quality standards. Job preference was given to those with the best quality records, and longer contracts were awarded to those with a continuing commitment to quality in the materials they supply Ford. In addition, the Quality Commitment Performance Program (QC-P) was launched to rate dealer service.

Evaluation

In 1987, the quality improvement effort at Ford was as much alive as it was in 1983. Now institutionalized in the company's *Mission, Values and Guiding Principles* and in a policy letter entitled "Ford Total Quality Excellence," a

key part of the effort has been the realization that productivity improvement can only come from improvement in
quality.

In recent years, greater emphasis has also been placed
on Total Quality Excellence (continual improvement of all
processes, not just in manufacturing) and on understanding the "voice of the customer."

Since 1980, the Ford team has improved domestic car
and truck quality by more than 60 percent, proving that
"doing it right the first time" is what achievement in industry is all about.

> *We've learned that the plan and its implementation need to be uniquely suited to your particular business and, as important, the specific financial objectives you have for it. . . . There is no magic, just good knowledge of your needs.*
> —Dr. Charles E. Cheeseman
> Senior Scientist

GE'S DAYTONA SIMULATION AND CONTROL SYSTEMS

Robots build simulation and control systems faster and better

The Program

Ten years ago computer-generated visual image systems were a high-tech specialty. Built mostly by hand, only about a dozen were produced each year. Since then, however, the demand for such systems has increased 700 percent, and GE needed to find a way to increase production while still maintaining its high quality standards.

GE's solution was to design its new Daytona plant as "the factory of the future." It contains a two-armed, light-assembly robot that can trim, form, and insert components, sense and discard damaged or inferior parts, and reduce programming time when adapting to minor variations in the printed wire board designs.

With its two x-y-z arms, the Daytona robot is capable of seven different motions. Special features permit it to transfer assemblies on and off the line and to gauge insertion force to prevent damage to components. Both arms operate simultaneously and do not have to stop for loading or unloading. A human operator can remove individual boards when completed and has only to supply parts and boards in response to the robot's needs.

Evaluation

The robot at GE's Daytona plant has significantly improved the manufacturing precision of visual image systems and greatly increased GE's production capabilities. It can assemble boards three and a half times faster than a human operator and its sensing capabilities have reduced errors and board defects by 42 percent.

*One other old dog has learned new tricks.
We've moved in computers, lasers, robots,
and a highly advanced handling system. It's
still an old building from the outside, but
inside those meters are pouring out.*
— Jules Mirabel
GE Technology Manager

GE'S METER AND CONTROL BUSINESS DEPARTMENT

GE converts old factory to high
productivity using computerized
materials handling and new addition on
the roof

The Program

At GE's meter plant in Somersworth, New Hampshire, increased production requirements had outstripped plant capacity. The need for outside warehouse space was imminent, but there was nothing available within a reasonable distance. To make matters worse, an inefficient materials transport system between floors that used freight and passenger elevators was very time consuming.

GE took the existing multi-floor structure and built a new addition on the roof. A sophisticated materials-handling system—one equally as efficient as those used in single-floor plants—was designed to include three automated storage systems and two conveyor networks. Raw materials, work-in-process, and finished goods are now handled separately, and materials can be requested from storage through data terminals on each assembly floor. An executive computer controls all three storage systems as well as the conveyor network that services the finished goods and work-in-process systems.

Special design features have also been added to increase productivity and space utilization. In the finished-goods system, for example, a conveyor loop with multiple spurs interconnects the adjacent unit-load and mini-load systems and interfaces with an automatic lift, which carries finished goods to the second floor.

Work-in-process materials are also controlled by computer. Inventories are called up when needed for assembly, and the appropriate toolboxes are distributed to the assembly floors by the conveyor network and automatic lifts.

Evaluation

The new computerized retrieval system at GE's Somersworth plant creates 40,000 square feet of storage space in the old building, 10,000 square feet more than would have been gained if an adjacent warehouse had been added— and at a lower cost. Before the new system was installed, 75 percent of a stockkeeper's time was spent traveling between storage sites, but now materials are brought over automatically. In addition, the computer system maintains a file on material location to keep track of the distribution and receipt of stock for operators.

> *Our locomotive plant in Erie is almost 70
> years old. We spent $300 million giving that
> plant an electronic heart transplant. I
> wonder if people think of brand-new
> factories when you talk about automation.
> Well, that's not necessarily the case.*
> —Joseph Podolsky
> Plant Manager

GE'S ERIE
LOCOMOTIVE PLANT

GE refurbishes 70-year-old industrial
plant, increasing productivity more than
240 percent

The Program

When it came to locomotives, GE realized that it was
slowly being squeezed out of the market. Its existing manufacturing technology was antiquated and its competitors
were already using high-tech equipment to produce a superior product. To meet the competition head-on, GE decided that nothing less than a total redesign of its
locomotive manufacturing system would do.

At the company's 70-year-old locomotive plant in Erie,
Pennsylvania, a motor frame flexible machining system
that uses nine unmanned machine tools was installed,
along with a parts-load station and an automatic material

transport system. Some of the more innovative features of these new technologies included:

1. Computer-directed carts that automatically distribute parts to each machine station
2. Cutting tools that can be changed by numerical controls
3. Coolant and chips that can be automatically removed
4. New machines that are so adaptable that they can be substituted for one another within the system

The plant's steel plate burning facility, which fabricates more than 25,000 tons of steel plate parts per year, was also fully automated. It featured:

1. CALMA interactive graphics system that automatically displays different-shaped parts specifically designed to fit each plate more precisely
2. A burn machine that can be programmed so that a crane with magnetic lifters automatically delivers two-ton plates from the storage facility to the machine table
3. A computerized numerical control plasma-arc burning system that can cut two plates at once using four cutting torches (and is capable of cutting up to 150 inches per minute)

Evaluation

As a return on its initial investment, GE saw overall productivity at the Erie plant increase by more than 240 percent with significant improvement recorded in both product quality and consistency. The company has since added another unit to the plasma burning system to handle two-thirds of the total plate burning load. This has had the effect of doubling the plant's output, providing a 100 percent increase in labor productivity and a savings in material costs of up to $400,000 a year.

People working at night pay a price in terms of mental and physical health. If we can make their lives easier, why shouldn't we?
— Preston Richey
Operations Manager

GREAT SALT LAKE MINERALS AND CHEMICALS CORPORATION

Shift schedules in tune with workers' circadian rhythms boost productivity and lessen fatigue in round-the-clock operation

The Program

During peak seasonal production at the Great Salt Lake Minerals and Chemicals Corporation, work was performed around the clock in three shifts. Employees changed to the previous shift every seven days, but changing that often had unwanted side effects: One in three workers was reported falling asleep on the job.

Preston Richey, manager of operations, decided to conduct an experiment in conjunction with Dr. Charles Czeisler and the Center for Design of Industrial Schedules at Harvard University, an expert on human circadian cycles (or internal "body clocks"). They divided the work force into two groups: One was to change schedules every seven days, as before, while the other was to change only every twenty-one days. Knowing that most body rhythms tend to lengthen in the absence of environmental time cues, they also changed the direction of rotation forward for all employees—from day to swing to night shift.

Under this new scheduling system, complaints about schedule changes dropped from 90 percent to 20 percent among those in the group that rotated every twenty-one days. Turnover, absenteeism, and family problems all declined, while health and morale improved and productivity increased 20 percent. The entire work force was soon changed to the new twenty-one-day schedule. "Four years ago, our goal was 1,000 tons of potash per day," says Richey. "Now 1,500 tons is average with the same work force."

The company has also spent considerable amounts of time and effort to educate supervisors on how to measure productivity and how to share this information in visual form with hourly workers so that they can gauge their own output on a weekly or daily basis.

Evaluation

The new schedule rotation program continues to have widespread acceptance among employees at the Great Salt Lake Minerals and Chemicals Corporation. Though potash operations were curtailed due to flooding of the pond system, all other operating areas in the company continue to show a 3 to 7 percent productivity improvement each year. Since one in four men and one in six women in the U.S. labor force work on variable schedules, this experiment highlights an unrecognized phenomenon that may have major implications for American industry.

We try to remember to demonstrate that
every job is important and each individual,
in carrying out his function well, is an
important contributor.

—Hewitt Associates Philosophy

HEWITT ASSOCIATES

Benefits consulting firm designs program
for employees juggling work and
parenting responsibilities

The Program

As a consulting firm that designs progressive compensation
and benefits programs for other companies, Hewitt Associates decided to help its own employees who are working
parents by providing the following assistance:

1. Maternity Return Options. In some cases, associates
who have recently had a child are allowed additional un-
paid time off or can return to work on a part-time basis for
a limited period. If there are special needs, the associate
can discuss the situation further with a manager to decide
whether the same or a similar job would be available after
an extended leave, and whether the job is one that can be
covered during the interim period by someone else.

2. Reimbursement for Overnight Babysitting. Hewitt
often provides reimbursement for overnight babysitting
costs to associates who must be out of town on business

overnight. Those who qualify must either be single parents or have a working spouse who is also out of town on business. This reimbursement does not include care provided by a live-in sitter or relative.

3. Salary Conversion Limit. Associates are permitted to convert as much as $4,800 from their yearly salary to a flexible compensation spending account to cover health-care and dependent-care expenses.

4. Sick Child Care. Hewitt has negotiated an arrangement with area hospitals that allow associates to reserve vacant pediatric beds when their children are not well enough to go to school. Costs vary from $30 to $40 and are the parent's responsibility. This program provides an additional option for parents whose day-care facilities cannot accommodate sick children.

5. Parent's Helper. The company employs a "Parent's Helper" to act as a reference and referral resource for employees with children. The Helper collects, evaluates, and shares information on child-care providers, dry cleaners, housekeeping agencies, and so on, and cuts down on the time working parents have to spend investigating these services.

Evaluation

Working parents, especially single parents and parents in dual-income families, suffer high levels of guilt and anxiety today about not spending enough time with their children and not spending enough time at their jobs. They feel strongly that it is their responsibility to do well at both parenting and working. In this regard, any psychological support, practical timesavers, and information resources that can be offered are greatly appreciated.

As a benefits consulting firm, Hewitt had developed a program that demonstrates creativity and resourcefulness in responding to the vast changes taking place in society, in the workplace, and in the integration of work and family life. It has shown that increased employee morale is achievable at a relatively low cost. And though it is hard to put a dollar figure on the benefits of the program, no one doubts that it has improved the company's ability to compete.

Above all, being more sensitive to the needs of working parents provides a way of showing that the company cares about its employees.

> *By establishing a far-reaching goal and getting people to feel in their gut that the goal was reasonable, we felt some serious movement would begin to occur. We also knew the close linkage between high quality, lower costs, and increased productivity would lead to other beneficial results for the company.*
>
> —John Young
> CEO

HEWLETT-PACKARD COMPANY

Total quality-control program achieves tenfold increase in reliability at major electronics firm

The Program

At Hewlett-Packard, as much as 25 percent of its manufacturing assets were tied up simply in mobilizing "reactions" to quality problems. Though quality standards were high, improvements were needed if the company was to maintain its leadership position in the electronics industry. So a new quality program was developed that went well beyond the quality circle concept to Total Quality Control (TQC).

The first step the company took in that direction was to establish a goal: to improve reliability by a startling 1,000 percent. Management felt that by setting such a difficult-to-reach objective employees would focus more on changing their basic approach to work and less on improving their old ways of doing things. "Perfection is the goal" became the company slogan and customer satisfaction the test of achievement.

Second, all senior managers were trained in quality-assurance techniques. Doing it right the first time was the principal lesson to be learned.

The third area of the program focused on stimulating employees to increase productivity. Newsletters, informal meetings, training classes, and over 1,000 quality teams were set up to accomplish this feat.

The fourth step involved instituting a computerized management information system. Research employees were guaranteed unlimited access to needed information data bases for experimentation, and programs were developed to track rework and parts failure data.

The fifth step was to encourage vendors and suppliers to participate in the TQC program. Involving the supplier, it was thought, would ensure quality parts and a quality product.

Finally, the TQC approach was expanded from manufacturing to other areas within the company, such as inventory control and accounts receivable.

Evaluation

As a result of the TQC program at Hewlett-Packard, quality and productivity have improved dramatically.

- Service and repairs on desk-top computers have dropped 35 percent through improved design and manufacturing techniques.
- Overall production time has been reduced—lowering the cost of the company's two most popular oscilloscopes by 30 percent—and product defects have declined substantially.

- Major improvements have been recorded in the quality of parts supplied by vendors participating in the TQC program.
- Inventory costs fell from 20.5 percent of sales in 1979 to 13.8 percent of sales in 1987, leading to savings of $542 million.
- Overdue receivables dropped to $218,000 within two years, meaning that $434,000 less is now invested in the company in the form of uncollected funds.

In 1987, the approach was extended to Hewlett-Packard's TQC strategic planning and implementation process. Management believes that this move may bring about even more breakthrough results than the application of TQC to any area of the company so far.

> *Together, we can find the answers.*
> —Company Motto

HONEYWELL INC.

Participative productivity programs proliferate, producing prodigious profits

The Program

From its initial Twin City Suggestion Plan for hourly workers—which has been in continuous operation since 1942—to the dozens of new programs and techniques now in operation, management in this labor-intensive organization has long focused on increasing productivity. Most recently, since 1987, the emphasis has been put on improving quality and productivity in white-color areas.

Honeywell's new "Winning Edge" program is a multi-tiered system of communications that enables employees to understand better how their contributions relate to the whole of the company. The "Strive for Error-Free Performance" (STEP) program stresses quality and the need to meet customer requirements precisely, while Value Analysis is being promoted in overhead and staff areas to measure productivity gains over time. The Aerospace and Defense Group's Productivity and Quality Center provides guidance and consultation throughout the company, encouraging productivity through both better communications and better internal competition. Extensive use is also being made of work-flow and input-output analysis.

More than 1,100 quality circles are now in place throughout the company, and the original suggestion plan has been extended to non-hourly workers, paying up to $2,500 per suggestion.

Evaluation

All these new programs at Honeywell have helped to produce an atmosphere in which employees work actively to improve productivity. The introduction of extensive automation and robotics has ignited little or no resistance from the work force. Energy use in the last decade has been reduced 34 percent, while total output has increased 65 percent. And $29 million has been saved through suggestion systems alone since 1975. In a recent survey, 70 percent of Honeywell's work force agreed with the statement that productivity improvement is everyone's responsibility.

> *Skilled, responsible management and superior productivity are inseparable. We are entering a far more demanding era requiring greater professionalism in management. Tomorrow's manager, in addition to being technically qualified in his or her field, must be a respected, people-oriented leader skilled in the latest techniques of behavior science and sound business practice.*
> —Robert Ranftl
> Retired Corporate Director

HUGHES AIRCRAFT COMPANY*

Managers learn how to improve personal and company productivity in one-day training session

The Program

Where *does* one find a "skilled, responsible manager"? Hughes Aircraft believes they are not found, but created. That is why management development has been a crucial part of this company's operations for many years.

Not long ago, a one-day management seminar was designed at Hughes by Robert Ranftl "to develop not only

---

* Now a division of General Motors.

understanding of productivity but a dedicated commitment to productivity improvement throughout our entire management team." At the outset of each seminar, Ranftl, now retired, would point out that "good managers do not fit the same mold—each one must use his or her own unique style" and that the purpose of the seminar was the "sharing of insights and a shopping list of ideas and productivity tools."

Now given hundreds of times, the seminar is today divided into four modules, each concentrating on a different facet of productivity. The first module reviews the "Anatomy of Productivity": Why is productivity important? What affects productivity? How does one evaluate productivity? And most important, how does one improve productivity? This kind of basic, primer approach is used so that the managers can return to their own unit or department after the seminar and have an immediate positive impact on the grass-roots level.

The second module in the seminar looks more closely at managerial and organizational productivity, focusing on the most common factors that aid or inhibit productivity improvement in companies across the nation. It also looks at the roles management must play in dealing with counterproductive factors, placing special emphasis on the role of leadership. "True leaders bring out the best in people and organizations," says Ranftl. "This is largely because leaders elicit strong positive emotional reactions, and because people tend to fulfill their needs and grow under effective leadership."

The third module deals with personal productivity, identifying a number of ways to combat counterproductive tendencies, while the fourth module identifies specific ways to improve productivity at Hughes. Here, the seminar group is divided into smaller subgroups, each of which brainstorms ways to overcome counterproductive factors within the organization. Their suggestions are then passed on to senior management, so that those in the upper echelons of the company can learn what their subordinates want to see done.

Evaluation

The seminar approach that is used at Hughes aircraft to develop managers may be somewhat unique, but it has been shown to be highly effective. And the popularity of the program continues to grow. It never fails to help managers to identify productivity inhibitors and to discover new ways to eliminate them.

> *Humana is state-of-the-art in terms of cost control and plans to be state-of-the-art in terms of providing medical technology.*
> —Robert Irvine
> Manager

HUMANA INC.

Central computer purchasing system results in savings of $85 million over three-year period

The Program

When Humana first began to expand rapidly, its managers could see that duplications in billing, purchasing, and staff could become very costly. So they decided to install a mainframe computer that would link all terminals throughout the hospital system and to implement a cost-reduction program that focuses on three major areas.

Billing. All patient bills and insurance forms are now fed through telephone lines at night to the main data-processing center in Louisville. Insurance companies and other health-care service vendors receive all their information—batch style—from this central facility.

Purchasing. The mainframe computer keeps track of supply levels at each Humana hospital, and all medical equipment is purchased through a central office. Buying supplies for 17,000 hospital beds allows Humana to take advantage of substantial volume discounts.

Staffing. Almost 60 percent of any hospital's operating costs are attributable to staffing. So at Humana, staffing requirements are based on departmental work load, as indicated by an automatic statistical gathering process that provides an analysis of the skill levels needed on any particular day. Taking into consideration the number of patients being treated, the computer then calculates each hospital's daily staffing requirements. A reserve corps of employees is on call twenty-four hours a day, seven days a week, and a special effort is being made to use lesser-skilled employees as often as possible and to reserve more highly skilled employees only for those times when they are truly needed.

In addition, Humana is constantly evaluating the efficiency of its support system to make sure its professionals are being properly served at all times. The financial and practical feasibility of contracting out some services—such as biomedical engineering or food plans—to other industry experts is also being evaluated on a regular basis.

Evaluation

Centralizing computer operations at a large health-care organization can prove to be highly cost effective. At Humana, the new billing procedures help speed up the receipt of revenues, and the purchasing program is on its way to achieving the expected $85 million of savings in three years.

Humana also estimates that its effort to closely monitor staffing levels gains the company a 5 percent cost advantage over other hospitals. For Humana, this equates to a savings of approximately $35 million a year.

> *Even though our products are untouched by human hands, you still have to have humans. You're going to have a better-quality product as long as the humans maintain the machine and do it properly.*
> —Nancy Mikaelian
> Executive Vice-President

HURON MACHINE PRODUCTS, INC.

Manufacturer implements employee training program to realize maximum yield from FMS investment

The Program

While other businesses were having problems making ends meet during the 1982–1983 recession, Huron Machine Products was investing heavily in flexible manufacturing systems (FMS), computer-aided design/computer-aided manufacturing (CAD/CAM), and computerized numerical control (CNC) systems to aid in its own design and manufacture of FMS components. But these high-precision manufacturing systems led Huron into a "people trap": the systems' sophistication exceeded the company's ability to use them efficiently. Some training was being provided by distributors, but Huron felt that to fully utilize these "new-age" products it would have to address the human operator factor.

So the company introduced a work team concept into its flexible manufacturing system. The objective was to motivate workers to improve their productivity by helping them understand what the new technology could do for them.

These work teams, which have been used for over seven years now, are set up according to work area, and meetings are run by regular employees who have been trained as facilitators. A facilitator's job is to coordinate the meetings, help generate ideas, mediate conflicts, and encourage positive thinking. Statistical quality-control techniques are reviewed during the meetings, charts and graphs are used to illustrate machine productivity and product quality, and intricate analyses are made to help plan short- and long-term production periods.

The basic rationale behind the program is to increase the flow of communication between management, the work force, and the computerized machinery. But the program also is being used to document and review the productivity levels of these new, high-tech manufacturing systems.

Evaluation

Huron's flexible manufacturing system operates twenty-four hours a day, seven days a week, using three twelve-hour shifts, each shift working four days on and four days off. After the introduction of the system in 1983, operators were able to improve the productivity of the company by 22 percent over 1982. Since then, Huron has experienced continued productivity improvement and expects still further improvement in the years to come.

There is another benefit: Due to a combination of efficiency and attrition, Huron has been able to reduce its work force requirement by 33 percent. As jobs are displaced due to increased efficiencies, employees are routinely retrained and reassigned. Attrition can be filled with retrained and reassigned personnel.

With its computer-controlled manufacturing systems, the company has also eliminated the need for rework and reduced re-setup time because any mistakes in initial setup are caught during simulated trial runs. Over the years, both the workers and engineers have learned to develop and utilize high-level skills to manage the company's sophisticated systems productively.

> *Intel needs to change. What worked in the*
> *past won't work in the future.*
> —from Intel 1986 strategic direction

INTEL CORPORATION

**Earlier productivity techniques become
a way of life while new techniques pay
off in a "meaner, leaner" organization**

The Program

After successful implementation of the Administrative Productivity Program, Intel's Productivity Group began a process to "make productivity a way of life, every day." This involved transferring its productivity techniques to line organizations. The group also created additional tools aimed at reducing administrative overhead and increasing management efficiency and effectiveness. The program had three main parts:

1. Task Simplification Training
2. Workload Distribution Analysis
3. Organization Structure Optimization

Task Simplification was incorporated as part of process improvement courses taught in division-level quality improvement programs called Quality Improvement Process, Continuous Process Improvement, and Employee Involvement. Due to the success of these new programs, a corporate-level task simplification class was discontinued in 1988.

Workload Distribution Analysis was developed to determine the amount of time being used in non-value-added
activities. These non-value-added activities were usually
tasks which employees had continued to do for a long time
without questioning their significance to the mission of the
organization. This analysis was applied to various groups
of about 10–50 employees. The analyses usually found 10
to 40 percent labor savings, which either were reassigned
to higher priority tasks or resulted in bottom-line reductions.

Organization Structure Optimization was instituted to
minimize the number of management levels within the
company and to increase the speed of communications.
Using a technique called "Spans and Levels," the entire
company organization of over 20,000 positions was analyzed. Overall, the group usually found that about 10 percent of all management positions could be eliminated or
combined with existing positions. This technique was used
during reorganizations in 1986 to save over $6 million and
to reduce more than two management levels. During 1986–
1988, the company reduced more than four management
levels. This technique was so successful that the group
eventually concentrated more than 80 percent of its efforts
to it in 1988.

Evaluation

During 1986–1988, Intel's Productivity Group documented
over $12 million in savings. Between 1986 and 1988, the
group moved more of its emphasis from lower-level task-
oriented analysis to higher-level organization structure optimization. The group changed its name in 1986 to the
Intel Internal Consulting Group.

In 1986, about 60 percent of the group's workload was
focused on organization structure; in 1987, 70 percent, and
in 1988, 80 percent. In 1988, a computer program was developed internally which could generate structure reports
from personal computer-based organization chart data-
bases. This allowed the analysis package to be transferred

to division-level personnel for their use. Organization structure analysis continues on a quarterly or semi-annual basis.

The Intel Internal Consulting Group was eliminated in 1989. In retrospect, its objectives had been met:

• Task Simplification Training and Workload Distribution (Value-Added) Analysis are now part of ongoing quality improvement processes.
• Organization Structure Optimization is automated and transferred to the line organizations for their use.

*Throughout its history, the JLM
Committee has served to open lines of
communication that are grounded in the
belief that new attitudes, trust, and risk-
taking can result in a better understanding
and appreciation of each other's
responsibilities and concerns.*
—Nicholas A. Fidandis
Chairman

JOINT LABOR
MANAGEMENT COMMITTEE,
RETAIL FOOD INDUSTRY

Structured cooperation between union
and management engenders trust,
stability, and foresight

The Program

The need for better cooperation between labor and management was recognized in the retail food industry during
the last era of wage and price controls, from 1971 to 1974.
The present Joint Labor Management Committee (JLMC)
of the Retail Food Industry was established in 1974 by vol-
unteer representatives from both management and labor,
partly as an outgrowth of the Tripartite Wage and Salary
Committee of the Cost of Living Council. As now consti-
tuted, the JLMC includes members from the three largest

unions in the industry and thirteen supermarket companies. These companies range in size from the largest operating in the United States and Canada to mid-size and
smaller regional chains, which altogether employ more
than 400,000 workers represented by the three member
unions. The JLMC is charged with improving collective
bargaining, preventing unnecessary strikes, promoting
long-range stability, and encouraging open and high-level
communication on various issues affecting the retail food
industry.

The JLMC is funded annually by both the unions and
the corporations, whose chief officers form the Executive
Committee. Under the direction of an impartial chairman,
the Executive Committee determines the issues to be ad-
dressed and sets policy guidelines for implementation by a
Steering Committee consisting of the corporate VPs of
labor and industrial relations and their union counterparts.
The Steering Committee meets on a near bimonthly basis
to discuss topics drawn from a pre-circulated agenda. Subcommittees are formed on an ad hoc basis to address specific topics of interest to the members.

Evaluation

The JLMC monitors all industry contracts about to expire
and offers to mediate settlements in key collective-bargaining situations. It has helped bring about peaceful settlements in five of eight disputes covering about 82,000
bargaining unit workers.

The JLMC has used its subcommittees to address specific work issues and has achieved some positive results.
Regulations affecting retail meat cutters formulated by
JLMC, for example, were adopted in their entirety by
OSHA, as were recommendations resulting from a five-
year JLMC-initiated study by the Harvard School of Public
Health on the possible effects of materials and working
conditions in retail meat departments. New policies stem-
ming from the impact of Universal Product Code (UPC)
technology were also developed.

The JLMC has published two studies on methods of containing health-care cost increases, both of which have been widely circulated: "Putting a Lid on Health Care Costs" (1980) and "A Joint Labor Management Communication on Health Care Cost Management" (1985). Other JLMC research has involved productivity measurement, unfunded liability of multi-employer pension funds and health and welfare plans, multi-tier wage settlements, alcohol and substance abuse, and data collection within the industry.

The work conducted by the JLMC has even greater significance now that sales in the retail foods industry have exceeded 10 percent of this country's gross national product and employment has reached nearly 3 million workers. It has proved over a long period of time (since 1974) that "working together" can provide benefits that "working as adversaries" cannot.

*It isn't easy to change. It's easier to do
things the way you've always done them.
It's easier to concentrate on "things" than
to try to understand and develop people.
But in a competitive, rapidly changing
marketplace, doing things the same old way
just won't do. We need to be creative,
innovative, and energetic.*

—Vern Lindstrom
President

KITCHELL CORPORATION

Comprehensive participative
management program helps to develop
new managers for future growth

The Program

Like many of today's top executives, president Vern Lindstrom of the Kitchell Corporation (which offers construction services) wanted to find a way to institutionalize the
entrepreneurial spirit that had helped his company grow
well beyond the small family firm that could communicate
easily within one office. He felt that the need to develop a
new kind of manager, in particular, was critical for the
success of this company's future expansion plans.

Lindstrom's solution was the People Management System, a plan he says will help Kitchell "to produce and communicate in a more efficient manner, provide proper
performance evaluation and recognition, and have more

employee participation in the management of the company." The system has already been integrated into the strategic plans for the company and includes a number of important components:

- An organizational structure designed for flexibility and growth
- Personnel planning to meet future needs
- A performance evaluation system
- An employee relations plan to meet employee needs for direction and recognition
- A companywide productivity plan
- A progressive compensation, incentive, and reward system
- A personnel administration system to monitor working conditions
- An employee communications plan
- A comprehensive marketing and sales system
- A computer integration plan

At first, Lindstrom had to hire a number of communications, education, and productivity directors to develop and coordinate all these programs. Using technical, political, and cultural change models, a flexible organizational structure for continued growth was implemented. Then employee communications were expanded and task forces developed to generate involvement and input and new computer technology was integrated into the company.

A performance evaluation system was set up that reinforces one-to-one relationships between employees and supervisors, and sets goals and performance standards that are reviewed quarterly. The system is also designed to identify areas where further training and education are needed —in an effort to develop the kind of management strength and depth that will be needed in the future.

Kitchell also utilizes a consultant to implement a program that it says will help the company's employees become more effective as individuals and as a team. Called Educational Development for Growth and Effectiveness, or EDGE, the program has been made available to all employees on a voluntary basis, as well as to their spouses and high-school-age children. The first part of the program, "Increasing Human Effectiveness," provides concepts, techniques, and skills necessary to prepare for a climate of active teamwork and cooperation. In order to promote consistently high performance and job satisfaction, a common language for goal setting and problem solving is also developed.

The second part of the program concentrates on team building and is specifically designed for the senior management group of each Kitchell company and for managers within individual departments. Here, teams of managers work to develop a mission statement with shared values and to establish a set of goals to add consistency to long-range planning. By having managers identify personal, departmental, and company values, and engage in trust-building exercises, the program helps them develop self-esteem and mutual respect within their groups.

The third and final aspect of the program is plan maintenance, which consists of periodic visits by consultants to monitor effectiveness of the program, assist individuals who are having implementation problems, and strengthen the team-building process where needed.

Evaluation

Although the Kitchell Corporation has not attempted formally to measure the results of its program, the company has improved its capture ratio for marketing, increased its sales volume, achieved higher profit margins, lowered turnover, and earned recognition within its industry, all since implementing various components of the People Management System. Employee feedback on the benefits of the program has been consistently positive, and overall employee morale has improved significantly.

Though it has been restricted by limited human and financial resources, and had to be phased in slowly over a four-year period, the People Management System has prompted a great deal of effort to restructure the company and to create a receptivity to change and willingness to innovate. Employee input so far has resulted in a number of significant systems improvements and some promising new concepts for improving productivity.

> *Workers should be paid on the basis of their accomplishments and efficiencies; they should share in the profits their efforts make possible.*
>
> —James F. Lincoln
> Founder

LINCOLN ELECTRIC COMPANY

Incentive system helps maximize both wages and profits for welding equipment manufacturer

The Program

The statement above, made by James F. Lincoln in 1952, still holds true at Lincoln Electric today. Workers are paid more when they help bring about work efficiencies, and they share in the profits of the company.

To accomplish the former, Lincoln attempts to operate as many jobs as possible on a straight piecework basis. Piece standards are permanently fixed and change only if a different method, material, or machine is introduced in any particular operation. Any worker who can figure out a way to produce above standard receives more pay and Lincoln does not limit the amount of money an employee can earn.

Employees are given a share of the company's profits through a bonus paid in a lump sum at the end of the fiscal year. (The company feels it is not possible to determine success on a shorter basis and still be fair to both share-holders and employees.) After a dividend is declared and the future cash needs of the company are taken care of, the balance is distrubuted among all employees at a rate, expressed as a percentage of base pay, that is determined by the board of directors.

BONUS EXAMPLE

Annual Wage Rate	Company Bonus Rate	Merit Rating of Employee	Computed Bonus	Total Compensation
$17,000	100%	85%	$14,450	$31,450
$24,000	100%	118%	$28,320	$52,320

All employees are reviewed for merit ratings twice each year, and in this process each employee is compared to other members of his or her merit rating group. Everyone is evaluated in four categories: ideas and cooperation, output, dependability, and quality. Merit ratings range between 80 and 120 percent.

Lincoln Electric feels that a compensation system that combines piecework with bonuses creates a strong motivating factor at both the individual and group levels. Employees feel they are competing with themselves, not their peers, and everyone knows that he or she has the same chance and opportunity to excel.

The system also encourages cooperation, because bonuses are tied directly to company profits. Peer pressure and individual feelings of accountability help ensure that everyone does his or her part. According to Harry Carlson, a company executive, "employees want to increase both the total pool and their cut of that pool."

Managers also play an an important role in enhancing the system by working to break down any and all barriers that may hinder individual performance. "Managers must allow latent abilities to come to the surface," says Carlson. "The whole idea is to give people the opportunity to do a better job today than they did yesterday."

Evaluation

At Lincoln Electric, employees are considered valuable assets and, as such, they are treated honestly, respectfully, and generously. The average bonus paid out in 1989 was $20,800. That year, some production employees earned over $90,000. The company imposes no mandatory retirement age, and guarantees all employees at least 30 hours of work each week. Even in the 1982 recession, no one was laid off.

Today, many companies embrace the slogan "Work smarter, not harder." But given the work ethic he helped develop in his own company, James Lincoln would probably have preferred the slogan "Work smarter and harder."

*Why an employee stock ownership plan?
It's the most dynamic, the most flexible
employee gainsharing plan I know of.*
—Robert Strickland
Chairman

LOWE'S COMPANIES, INC.

Employees in specialty retail chain work
for themselves through employee stock
ownership plan

The Program

Motivating employees by giving them a stake in their company is not a new technique. For years, employee stock ownership plans (ESOPs) have been used as effective vehicles for sharing financial benefits among all those who contribute to bringing them about. One of the oldest and most successful ESOPs in the country is the one at Lowe's Companies, Inc.

Lowe's ESOP story is a truly dynamic one. In 1975, *Newsweek* featured an article describing a Lowe's employee who had never earned more than $125 a week but who retired with $660,000 in Lowe's stock. Like all Lowe's employees, he did not have to contribute a penny of his personal funds to buy the stock, because each year the company puts aside up to 15 percent of its payroll to be invested in its ESOP plan.

Lowe's chairman Robert Strickland is the program's most enthusiastic spokesperson. He will tell anyone that, without a doubt, the company's ESOP plan has been a key ingredient of its success.

> How do I know it works? How do I know that Lowe's growth wasn't influenced more by geography, or the business we're in, or management skill? Because in the late 1950s and early 1960s there were at least five other companies just like ours in the Sunbelt: one in Virginia, one in South Carolina, one in Florida, and two in North Carolina. The same geography, the same business—different management, of course, but not bad management. Three of the companies didn't make it on their own and sold out. The fourth company is about one-fourth our size and has just adopted an employee stock ownership plan. It was a case of survival of the most motivated and the most productive.

One question many people ask about ESOPs is: What happens to employee motivation when the price of the company stock drops? According to personnel director Ed Spears, no one at Lowe's seems to mind. Employees there are sophisticated enough to understand that the conditions

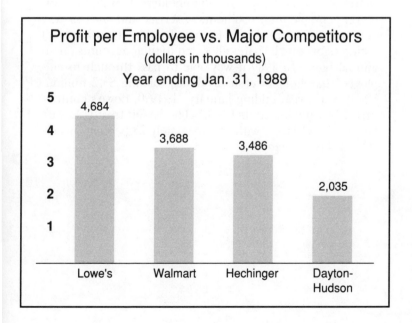

Profit per Employee vs. Major Competitors
(dollars in thousands)
Year ending Jan. 31, 1989

Lowe's	4,684
Walmart	3,688
Hechinger	3,486
Dayton-Hudson	2,035

that cause stock prices to fluctuate are usually temporary. Some even look forward to an occasional price drop because they realize that the company can then purchase more stock than it could at a higher price. The October 1987 stock market crash, for instance, gave employees just such an opportunity and they took advantage of it.

The ESOP plan at Lowe's is now an integral part of the company's identity. Employees like it because it provides them with a substantial financial package for their retirement, and management likes it because it helps keep the work force highly motivated and productive.

Evaluation

Lowe's ESOP program has been such a continuing success that in February 1990 the company released the following information:

> Lowe's is extremely proud of its ESOP, which has proven to be an outstanding asset for its company, its employee shareholders, and its other shareholders as well. All employees completing 1,000 hours of service and one full year of employment are eligible for membership. They have full voting rights on all shares allocated to their accounts on an annual basis. In 1989 it was able to pass through to employee shareholders cash dividends totaling $3.2 million. For its fiscal year ending January 31, 1990, Lowe's contributed $22.1 million to its ESOP. The ESOP trust is Lowe's largest shareholder, with approximately 25 percent ownership of the company.

> *The payroll savings helped us through a*
> *tough time for the company, and kept*
> *everyone in a job.*
>
> —Linda Steel
> Personnel Director

McCREARY TIRE & RUBBER COMPANY

Distributing layoffs through furlough
rotation helps tire manufacturer cut
direct labor costs and shift into new lines
of production

The Program

Like a lot of other companies trying to weather the recession of 1982, McCreary Tire & Rubber Company was losing money—the recession had dramatically reduced demand for its passenger tires. As part of a long-range plan to cut costs and shift to manufacturing truck and specialty tires, the company decided to implement a rotating furlough system instead of laying off a large portion of its work force.

Each week, one-third of the company's 400 production workers were "laid off" on a rotating basis. Each employee would work for two weeks and then, under an agreement with the state of Pennsylvania, collect supplemental payments for less than full-time employement during the third week, when the employee would be on furlough. In this way, every McCreary employee was able to work two of every three weeks through the summer of 1982, as the troubled company shifted into a more profitable production line.

Evaluation

Even though the rotating furlough system has the effect of increasing a company's future payroll taxes, it did save jobs for workers at McCreary and helped the company survive the 1982 recession. In addition, productivity rose, absenteeism fell, on-the-job injuries decreased, and employee relations improved, at least in the short term.

The McCreary study ends on a less positive note, however. In March 1983 the company union went out on strike for about six weeks, and the furlough program was shelved. As the Pennsylvania economy improved during the next few years, job security was increased and employees forgot about the problems they had experienced during the summer of 1982.

But in March 1986 the company union went out on strike again, and McCreary replaced all its unionized employees with non-union workers or new hires. This dispute was never settled and a decertification election was held by the National Labor Relations Board in March 1988, when McCreary's employees voted 181 to 5 against joining the union.

Today, McCreary says it still believes in the rotating furlough system and would certainly reinstate it should the Pennsylvania economy experience another recession. It was a good idea, the company reminds us, but like all such plans, it is not a panacea.

*Motorola has evolved to its present state by
a determination to manage our physical,
financial, and human resources more
effectively and efficiently than before.*
—Ralph Ponce DeLeon
Manager

MOTOROLA, INC.

Electronics manufacturer initiates
participative management program that
gives everyone a chance to improve the
business

The Program

Motorola, a company of over 90,000 employees, has always
sought to remain as decentralized as possible while still
maintaining the financial welfare of the entire organization. Every profit center is run as if it were a separate company, each with its own engineering and marketing
departments, all in an effort to retain a small-company,
entrepreneurial, proprietary atmosphere.

At Motorola, the determination to improve its competitive position and its productivity took the form of a companywide effort called the Participative Management
Program (PMP), and PMP is a natural extension of company's policy of decentralization. It works by breaking
down each operating unit into logical teams whose sole
purpose is to make every employee a key contributor to
serving the customer better, and thus improving the suc-

cess of the business. Under the rules of PMP, each team is given a set of performance goals, and if these goals are met and the company meets its overall return on net assets target, a bonus is paid to each team member.

Any employees who are not commissioned salespeople or participants in the Executive Incentive Program can take part in PMP. The goals for PMP are set by a steering committee, which bases its decisions on both strategic operating and human resource considerations, such as: (1) quality, (2) current costs, (3) delivery, (4) inventory, (5) housekeeping and safety, and (6) cost reduction. All goals are quantified so that they can be easily measured on a regular basis, and every team conducts a monthly session to determine how well it is doing in meeting them.

Bonuses are distributed when a team meets its own goals, the profit center it belongs to achieves the pre-tax profit it had planned, and the entire company meets its overall profit target. (The company added the overall company profitability requirement in 1988 to make sure that decentralization does not lead to destructive internal competition.) When all three conditions are met, a portion of the profit earned is made available for bonuses, with the amount paid to each participant determined by that person's share of the team's total payroll.

As with most productivity programs, management's role has been key to the success of PMP, and at Motorola its most important job has been to create the kind of environment and atmosphere in which every person can contribute the most of what he or she has to offer. The backing and blessing of top management have also helped. In a recent speech, vice-chairman and chief operating officer William J. Weisz told his audience that PMP is now and will continue to be one of the most important contributors to Motorola's success:

> We believe that participative management, together with our fundamental policy of continuous decentralization, will make it possible to lead and work our behemoth successfully and artfully in the eighties and beyond. PMP is a

counterbalancing force to size, breaking challenges down to where individual employees can see the results of their participation.

Training has also been a strongly emphasized aspect of the program. And Motorola's philosophy is to provide the kind of training that encourages employees to understand the relationship between quality, productivity, and customer service, and to instill in them a basic understanding of "what our customers mean." This type of training is essential for the program to succeed, says management, because everyone's job is interrelated to everyone else's and it is important that all Motorola employees learn to think as a team.

Evaluation

Since PMP was initiated in 1968, Motorola's employees have had a strong voice in how their company is run, and that has helped keep morale and product quality at a high level. The company also believes that PMP has helped it "to provide the customer with the best possible product and service, in compliance with the customer's delivery schedule, at the lowest possible cost."

Although it is against company policy to release specific financial figures, Motorola says that PMP continues to bring about widespread cost savings, along with improvements in employee health and safety, and has helped the company successfully weather the economic turbulence of the 1980s.

> *I went through two Toyota assembly plants and a stamping plant in Japan and they have a fast pace. But their system is laid out so that it's easier for the worker to do the job than it is here.*
>
> —Bruce Lee
> Manager

NEW UNITED MOTOR MANUFACTURING INC.

UAW joins Japanese management in manufacturing small cars in California; will it work?

The Program

When Japanese imports began to account for a sizable share of the huge California automobile market, the General Motors Corporation and Toyota decided to work together to produce both Japanese and American cars in the United States. Together they converted a former GM assembly plant in Fremont, California, into a new company that would produce 650 Chevy Novas and Toyota Corollas a day using only unionized labor. Today 85 percent of the plant's former workers hold jobs in this new company called New United Motor Manufacturing Inc. (NUMMI).

If NUMMI can succeed in producing cars to Japan's high quality standards and with a unionized American work force, the venture could force profound changes throughout the U.S. auto industry. NUMMI has agreed to hire only furloughed workers from UAW's Local 1364 (now Local 2244) and has agreed to a no-layoff policy unless the fundamental, long-term viability of the company is jeopardized. In return, the UAW has agreed to accept NUMMI as a new venture not bound by seniority rights, work rules, or rigid job classifications. A Japanese-style management system has been put in place.

All assembly workers at NUMMI have a single job classification and are organized into work teams of five to seven people, each of whom is cross-trained in all team jobs. Skilled tradespeople are divided into only three classifications—tool and die, tool and die tryout, and maintenance —and all maintenance personnel are trained to work in all skill areas (electricity, metal plumbing, etc.).

The organizational hierarchy within the company consists of just six layers:

1. Team members
2. Leaders of teams with four to six members (nonsupervisory)
3. Group leaders with three teams
4. Assistant managers
5. Managers
6. Executive officers (vice-president for engineering, vice-president for quality control, vice-president for manufacturing, and president)

Management responsibility lies primarily with the teams, and only five layers of Japanese and American managers supervise the entire plant—one or two layers less than the typical U.S. plant—and with fewer managers at each level.

Since U.S. workers are used to receiving higher wages than their Japanese counterparts, NUMMI has worked to keep its labor costs down by adopting HMO health care and a nontraditional defined-contribution pension plan.

Evaluation

Production at NUMMI began in December 1984, and its performance standards were set for higher quality and lower cost. So far, results in both areas have exceeded the company's original expectations.

Today, NUMMI-produced cars are widely recognized as high-quality vehicles. They are repeatedly ranked well above average by independent automotive magazines, and in numerous surveys the Nova has come out number one in production quality among all American-made cars.

In addition, the quality of cooperation between management and labor at NUMMI now serves as a model not only for the auto industry, but for U.S. business in general.

The BME's experience belies the common notions that government workers cannot be as productive as their private-sector counterparts or that the output of a governmental operation cannot be measured. There is no simple formula for succeeding in the change from a traditional approach to the labor/management approach. It must begin with a critical factor—management's commitment to share its power with labor and some degree of imagination in devising accurate, but nonthreatening, ways to measure productivity. But given the effort and the true desire to see it succeed, it does work.

—Ron Contino
Deputy Commissioner

NEW YORK CITY DEPARTMENT OF SANITATION

Employee participation program transforms New York City bureau into "profit center"

The Program

When Ron Contino was appointed deputy commissioner for support operations in 1978, the Bureau of Motor Equipment (BME) in New York City's Department of Sanitation was widely regarded as being in a state of total chaos. Responsible for the largest municipal fleet of vehicles in the country, the BME has 1,200 employees, seven major central repair facilities, and seventy-three satellite repair garages throughout the five boroughs. Almost half of its sanitation trucks were unavailable on any given day, overtime was excessive and growing, and substantial rework was all too common.

Contino turned the BME around by using a two-part program of reform. After winning top management support, he organized permanent, full-time union/management committees to address the problems employees were having in performing their work. Then he abolished individual work standards and began to measure output only at the whole shop level. This, he believed, would help ensure that no employee labored at tasks that were unproductive and would provide the kind of peer pressure that would help the BME operate at the same level of efficiency as the private sector.

The Management Information System Contino had installed to monitor the progress of the program was also truly unique. It allows the bureau to calculate the costs of the various activities it performs and to compare those costs to the prices charged for the same services by vendors in the private sector. If repairing a transmission, for example, costs less for the bureau to do itself than to purchase, it will be retained as a job within the BME. But if it is determined that the service can be performed more cheaply by an outside vendor, the BME will shift its efforts to other work areas where it can be more productive. This aspect of the program was modified in 1986 to allow other city departments to submit bids for BME jobs—such as the fire department for emergency services. The newest program is a joint venture with the private sector to develop a new type of tire for New York's municipal fleet. Any savings that accumulate from the venture will be returned to the civil service work force through improvements in the quality of their work environment.

Evaluation

By turning the BME into a "profit center" and by promi-
nently displaying its productivity gains, Contino has helped
focus everyone's efforts toward achieving the kinds of results that will be felt citywide. The city comptroller has
recommended use of the programs in other city areas.

One of BME's components is a landfill operation; suggestions for this alone have resulted in a realized annual cost
avoidance of $114,000 and a proected annual cost avoid-
ance of $155,000. These included design modifications to
equipment needed to reduce downtime and plans to save
money by manufacturing in-house expensive repair parts
that would normally be purchased from outside vendors.

Overall, the eight shops involved in Contino's program
are operating at a "profit-center" productivity of 1.30,
which means that every dollar invested in them by the city
is producing goods and services that would cost $1.30 if
purchased from the private sector. In 1988, that translated
into an annual "profit" for the BME of $3 million.

> *Those managements which require rigid patterns of conformance are depriving the company of new ideas, better ideas, and innovations.*
>
> —F. Kenneth Iverson
> Chairman and CEO

NUCOR CORPORATION

New steel technology results in lower manufacturing costs

The Program

In 1970, most U.S. steel manufacturers relied on the costly ingot processing method to make their steel products. First, hot metal had to be poured into ingots, then it was reheated and rolled into billets for shaping. Time consuming and resource intensive, this process could take up to two weeks to complete. To achieve a competitive edge, Nucor decided to use a new technology based on continuous casting.

In the continuous-casting process, selected scrap iron and alloy elements are melted together and then poured into a continuous-casting billet system. The high pre-heat temperature in the ladle and a sliding gate valve permit a constant flow of liquid steel that is directly converted into billets, thereby eliminating all the cooling, reheating, and rolling that was once required with ingots.

Quality control at Nucor is also an important factor throughout the continuous-casting process. Samples are tested for chemical ratios, yield, tensile strengths, and elongation, and a computer is used to determine whether the tested materials conform to standard.

Evaluation

Nucor remains one of the most profitable steel firms in America, and the continuous-casting process is the principal reason for its success. It has increased the company's capacity, reduced its material and energy costs, and substantially lowered the prices the company must charge customers for its finished products. The ongoing search for new manufacturing methods has kept Nucor up-to-date and competitive with companies around the world.

> *The real art of management lies in the maximum utilization of ordinary men and women. Since these are always in plentiful supply, long-term success will go to those who know how to release the energy, zest, and hidden potential in us all.*
>
> —John G. Quay
> Training and Development Specialist

PALATINE POLICE DEPARTMENT

Dual-career ladder offers police officers higher earnings for expanded competence and increases departmental productivity

The Program

Bringing out the "hidden potential" in employees can be a difficult task. But the police department in Palatine, Illinois, has been able to do it through an innovative career advancement program called Dual Career Ladder (DCL).

The DCL was developed because the traditional career ladder that existed for police officers in Palatine was failing to address many of their frustrations and concerns. Though many officers were motivated by the promise of advancement, the structure of the department actually restricted such upward movement and provided few promotional opportunities. Nor did the system recognize and reward officers whose performance was superior to that of their peers or identify those officers whose performance was below standard. Finally, the system clearly lacked career alternatives for police officers who wanted to make more money but still wanted to remain "on the street."

After three years discussing the merits and possible effectiveness of the DCL, the Board of Trustees formally committed itself to the program and presentations were made to all department personnel. A task force was assigned to transform the concept into a working program and five subcommittees were established to examine specific topics; any police officer who was interested in a topic could become a member of the subcommittee that dealt with it.

The DCL works essentially by expanding the concept of lateral mobility. Any officer can make a lateral move as long as he or she meets several program requirements. These include: (1) at least one year at the top of his or her current pay classification, (2) proficiency in twenty-five knowledge and skill areas, (3) proficiency in a number of advanced skill and knowledge areas (the number depending on the pay level desired), (4) continuing education course work (the amount depending on the hiring date of the officer), and (5) satisfactory maintenance of overall job performance standards (measured by the number of tickets written, the number of criminal arrests made, and so on).

Each lateral "advancement" includes a pay bonus, identifiable insignia, recognition by the department, and increased job responsibility. After a year in the new job, the officer is required to pass through the selection process again in order to retain his or her position or advance to a new one.

Evaluation

Developed without the assistance of any federal dollars, the DCL has been able to increase productivity at the Palatine Police Department by almost 10 percent. Over the years, it has been modified and other programs have been added, but it still remains a vital mechanism for maintaining morale and ensuring top-flight performance.

Though they were developed solely by and for the use of the Palatine Police Department, the concepts and structures of the Dual Career Ladder program may prove useful in many nongovernmental organizations that are also dealing with the problems created by traditional—and perhaps antiquated—career-advancement systems.

PENNTAP

Costly technical assistance and
information available to businesses free

The Program

In 1965, the state of Pennsylvania decided to help its
200,000 small businesses acquire the technical, scientific,
and engineering know-how they would need in order to
prosper and remain competitive. So a partnership was established between Pennsylvania State University and the
state Department of Commerce to provide a public service
called PENNTAP—Pennsylvania Technology Assistance
Program.

PENNTAP may be used by any business owner, operator, or representative in Pennsylvania who has a problem
simply by contacting the main office in University Park or
any one of the twenty-seven other commonwealth offices.
One of PENNTAP's part-time specialists will be assigned to
the problem and may assist the user by offering suggestions
based on personal experience, consultations with other
PENNTAP specialists or Penn State faculty members, library or computer research, or an investigation into federal
resources. When all the information on the problem is assembled, it is usually presented to the user in the form of

several possible solutions, and always in understandable terms.

For their part, users are asked only to complete an evaluation form at some time in the future when the results of their contact with PENNTAP can be measured.

Evaluation

Through the end of 1988 PENNTAP had provided $123 million worth of economic benefits to Pennsylvania's economy at a cost of about $7 million—a cost-benefit ratio of 17 to 1. In addition, PENNTAP is credited with 49 new job opportunities and 27 new products developed in Pennsylvania in 1988. The number of individual public and private problems solved continues to grow.

Though few businesspeople are aware of it, the U.S. government will also provide businesses with direct access to virtually every aspect of unclassified government research—free of charge—simply by contacting the U.S. government's federal laboratories. Specific referrals can be made by the U.S. Office of Science and Technology Policy, Washington, D.C. 20506, telephone (202) 395-3000.

> *Our organization has set a course for*
> *productivity growth which is based on*
> *quality products and our people's desire to*
> *perform.*
> —Bruce Los
> Development Manager

PRINCE CORPORATION

Pay-for-performance program helps auto-
parts manufacturer evaluate employees
more objectively

The Program

The Prince Corporation wanted to establish a more direct
correlation between the productivity of its workers and
their pay. So the company developed a sophisticated pay-
for-performance program that evaluates each employee's
work performance in five different areas: (1) attendance, (2)
quality, (3) quantity, (4) cooperation, and (5) work rules.
Each Prince employee receives a numerical score for each
of the five areas, and the employee's hourly wage is directly
tied to the total score achieved. Work performance reviews
are conducted on a quarterly basis for the first three years
of employment with the company and on an annual basis
every year thereafter.

What happens when an employee's score drops? He or
she is given another three months to bring the score to its
previous level, but if it does not return, the employee's
hourly pay rate is adjusted downward. Prince's philosophy

is that everyone should be held accountable for his or her own actions—and rewarded accordingly—and the program has become such an integral part of the company's overall operations that president John Spoelhof reviews evaluations periodically to make sure the evaluators are doing their job.

Grading employees in the areas of attendance, quantity, and adherence to work rules is relatively easy but it may be a lot trickier for a supervisor to evaluate an employee's quality and cooperation. So all employees at Prince are expected to audit the quality of their own work using an objective rating system, and to post the results daily. This evaluation technique produces two important benefits for the company: It confirms management's belief in the integrity of each employee, and it provides each employee with immediate feedback on those areas that need improvement.

Another important part of Prince's pay-for-performance program is its bonus system. Distributed once a year, bonuses are based on (1) the corporation's overall profitability, (2) each division's profitability, and (3) each employee's work performance. Such a system, says Spoelhof, allows employees to feel that they work for themselves *and* that they are part of a team, which helps "build responsibility within themselves, their division, and the corporation."

Evaluation

Prince measures the success of its pay-for-performance system in terms of customer satisfaction. The company has received top-notch ratings from each of the major auto makers it serves and that has helped it enjoy remarkably steady growth. In addition, pay-for-performance fits very well within the company's overall corporate philosophy: "mutual trust and respect."

> We decided to pay people a weekly salary
> with the amount determined by the
> number of different jobs an individual
> could perform. There would be no time
> clocks or watchmen.
>
> —Stan Holditch
> Retired Plant Manager

THE PROCTER & GAMBLE COMPANY

Job enlargement plan based on pay-for-skills program and delegation of responsibility creates P&G's most productive plant

Background

The Procter & Gamble Company (P&G) has a long history of innovative employee recognition programs: Profit sharing was introduced in 1887, a Guaranteed Employment Plan was adopted in 1923, and a comprehensive employee benefits program was instituted in 1930. P&G's pay levels were high and its vacation benefits were generous, yet the company was not satisfied with the general levels of employee relations, motivation, and productivity.

What management sensed as an undercurrent of disgruntlement was being reflected in conflicts with workers over the administration of incentive pay and the standards used to determine compensation. New technology was being resisted with slowdowns and grievances, and productivity was declining and costs rising because many operations were trying to beat the "incentive system."

Recognizing the need to resolve these problems before they caused further damage to the company, its employees, and its customers, P&G assembled a task force of managers and experts drawn from all areas of the company and charged it with the responsibility of coming up with some solutions. The general conclusions reached by this task force were that P&G's employees would perform better if their job assignments included the following:

1. Greater responsibility for making decisions and for taking actions that affect their personal future

2. More diverse tasks of sufficient scope to provide greater challenges and a sense of accomplishment

3. More accountability for planning and executing their work assignments and for evaluating their work once it is completed

4. The opportunity to learn new skills and to experience personal growth on the job

5. Recognition from their peers and superiors for playing an important part in meeting company goals and in setting personal performance standards

The Program

To test the conclusions reached by the task force, the decision was made to apply these new concepts in a completely new plant that was being planned for Lima, Ohio, which would make consumer household products. The concepts were applied in the following ways:

1. The plant was organized into production teams, each responsible for operating a major part of the plant on its shift.

2. Each production team was composed of process technicians, packing technicians, and warehouse technicians, who together were responsible for the product from raw materials to final shipment and accounting.

3. Production team members were salaried personnel, and salary levels were determined by the number of different jobs an individual could perform.

4. The number of managerial positions in the plant was reduced to only one-fifth of those in a comparable P&G manufacturing facility. No time clocks or production overseers were used.

5. Clerical, laboratory, and other specialist positions were eliminated, while maintenance and clean-up jobs were contracted out.

6. Equipment was designed according to specific process needs and maintenance saving features were added whenever possible.

Evaluation

The Lima, Ohio, plant started operations in 1967 and quickly became a model for other new or converting P&G plants. Although start-up was challenging both for the plant's workers and for corporate management, the Lima facility achieved its projected targets within only one year. By the end of the first year, in fact, it was:

- First in production volume of any plant in the company, filling as many as seventy-five railroad cars a day with the output of fewer than 200 people
- First in quality production within the company
- Operating at lower costs than comparable plants within the company (and after four years operating at 40 percent of the cost of other P&G plants)
- Able to remain in operation during a two-day blizzard that paralyzed production at other midwestern plants
- Successful in modifying its packing lines to permit the use of new bottles (designed by a plant technician, not an engineer or manager, who in six months organized and implemented the changes required)·
- Able to solve numerous problems arising from the pur-

chase of bottles not uniform in size or according to specification, with the visit of a plant technician to the bottle manufacturer (where her meetings with management and machine operators resulted in a marked improvement in bottle quality)

Although this job-enlargement approach to motivating employees works in old facilities as well as new ones, P&G's experience indicates that newer production environments, with more modern layouts, more advanced equipment, and a new work force, can contribute to producing quicker and more certain results.

> *If we were going to keep the AFL-CIO alive, we had to keep the AFL-CIO contractors in business. You just begin by taking the first step.*
>
> —Richard Mantia
> AFL-CIO Executive

PRODUCTIVITY AND RESPONSIBILITY INCREASE DEVELOPMENT AND EMPLOYMENT (PRIDE)

Construction industry cooperation succeeds in St. Louis, leads to similar efforts across the United States

The Program

Back in 1972, St. Louis had a notorious reputation as a difficult trade union city. Jurisdictional strikes were closing construction sites several times a month, local businesses were delaying expansion because of the tensions, the number of labor hours worked was falling, and open shops were gaining contracts. Both union and construction leaders realized that unless serious changes were made, neither of them was going to survive.

It was then that leaders of the Building and Construction Trades Council decided to sit down with the Associated

General Contractors in an attempt to improve the city's construction climate. Together with the input of architects, engineers, and material suppliers, they drew up a "memorandum of understanding" called PRIDE—Productivity and Responsibility Increase Development and Employment. Based on the concept of compromise, its goals were to increase construction productivity, development, and employment within the St. Louis area. Union work rules were eased, featherbedding was eliminated, jurisdictional strikes were banned, and on-site management control was strengthened. Nonbinding arbitration through PRIDE was established in return for a no-picket-line pledge during contract strikes, and city contractors agreed to employ only union labor.

Perhaps the most important achievement of PRIDE, however, was preventive. In an attempt to improve productivity, and to resolve burgeoning problems before they became serious, monthly meetings of PRIDE were set up to evaluate the status of the construction industry in St. Louis on a continuing basis.

Evaluation

Even though PRIDE had no paid staff (two-thirds of its $7,000 budget was funded by contractors and one-third by its union members), it worked! Construction in the St. Louis area was rejuvenated—overall productivity rose between 10 and 15 percent—and trade union membership reached full employment. Within a short time, 98 percent of the city's commercial and industrial construction and 96 percent of its residential construction were being built with AFL-CIO labor. Projects were being completed in time and under budget, and all parties were benefiting from this cooperative effort at boosting productivity.

The success of PRIDE in St. Louis has already spawned at least ten similar programs around the country. These include MOST (Management and Organized Labor Striving Together) in Columbus, Ohio; PEP (Planning Economic Progress) in Beaumont, Texas; Union Jack in Denver, Colorado; and Top Notch in Indianapolis, Indiana.

> *The Company should be organized and*
> *conduct its affairs in such a manner as to*
> *make, as nearly as possible, each*
> *individual's work situation akin to what it*
> *would be if he or she were working for*
> *himself or herself.*
>
> —John May
> Director of Education and Training

THE PRUDENTIAL INSURANCE COMPANY OF AMERICA

Job redesign increases employee
motivation and results in a 53 percent
quality improvement

The Program

It was sometime during the 1960s when the Prudential Insurance Company realized that the proliferation of poorly designed clerical jobs within the company was frustrating its attempts to attract and retain high-quality employees. To combat this situation, the president announced his intention to develop the kind of "work environment that should encourage every Prudential man and woman to work creatively."

As a start, the company administered a lengthy employee survey to measure job attitudes and pinpoint areas where job design would do the most good. Then, an experimental effort was initiated in the ten home offices, the early results of which indicated that it would be advisable to implement the program companywide. The program had three main objectives:

1. To improve productivity, reduce error rates, and improve service
2. To raise the level of job satisfaction on a long-term basis
3. To make job design an integral part of management strategy

To ensure the success of the program, the Prudential developed a seven-point implementation strategy that included:

1. Establishing regional and home office task force teams
2. Training and developing job design consultants
3. Publishing a 400-page "how-to" manual for the consultants as a training tool and reference guide
4. Appointing a job design consultant to each Prudential office
5. Conducting workshops for all those who would be involved in job redesign in their areas
6. Conducting special training workshops for computer programmers in each office
7. Creating a training session for the Prudential auditing staff on job design concepts

Evaluation

In 1984, the consolidation of work brought about by the Prudential's job redesign effort made it possible for the company to reduce the number of its regional offices from eight to four. In addition, the program is credited with raising service levels 60 percent, improving quality by 53 percent, and boosting morale 61 percent. More than 90 percent of the company's managers felt that the job redesign effort has met or exceeded their original expectations of it.

Today, job redesign at the Prudential is no longer considered a special "program." It has become an integral part of the company's way of life, and all new jobs are designed with the needs of the employees in mind. What is more, the motivation behind this effort to design more satisfying and more creative jobs has spread to other areas of the company and has resulted in the development of quality circles, productivity improvement groups, organizational climate assessment techniques, career development efforts, and new training programs for performance appraisal systems.

> *An important thing to remember is that a crucial purpose of associations is to help companies save on freight costs. Unfortunately, many businessmen don't even know they exist.*
>
> —Claude Wooten
> Manager

SHIPPERS' ASSOCIATIONS

Shippers' associations pool cargo to reduce freight charges

The Program

For years businesspeople from all industries have formed special associations to consolidate their transportation needs and save money through volume shipping. In today's deregulated transportation environment, the expanded use of these associations is even more of a cost saver. Negotiated freight rates have become the norm, and a shippers' association can provide continuous, high-volume traffic.

Whether an association is industry specific (such as the carpet shippers' association) or handles a wide variety of goods, it works by pooling compatible cargoes with similar destinations into full truckload shipments, thus sparing many companies the higher fares they would have to pay for less-than-full loads. Further savings are also available for longer distances when associations take advantage of the "trailer-on-flatcar" or "container-on-flatcar" options provided by many railroads.

The passage of the Shipping Act of 1984 made it possible for the first time for shippers' associations to negotiate service contracts with ocean carriers. As a result the same benefits that have accrued to association members in their domestic freight arrangements are now available to them worldwide.

Evaluation

Though savings vary depending on geographic location and shipping volume, any company that belongs to a shippers' association can expect savings of at least 10 percent in its shipping costs, and some companies have recorded savings as high as 50 percent. Shippers' associations are well protected by existing laws and are not considered in violation of any antitrust laws in their normal course of activities.

More than 150 shippers' associations are currently functioning within the United States and new associations are being organized all the time. As long as either a shipper or a receiver is a member of a shippers' association, both parties may take advantage of the cost savings that are offered.

> *There is a bit of irony in the fact that the software industry, which specializes in automating other technologies, has been slow in automating its own critical processes.*
>
> —Leon Presser
> President

SOFTOOL CORPORATION

New computer program for data centers and programmers improves the quality of the software they produce and increases productivity

The Program

The information that is stored in computers is constantly going through change cycles that lead to new versions. Yet the inability to manage and control these changes is recognized as the single most serious obstacle to the effective utilization of computers today. It is a problem that is faced continually by software managers, developers, and users.

The Softool Corporation has become a leader in the development of a new computer discipline called "change and configuration management," which provides for the orderly review, testing, approval, and integration of changes like these. "Change management" helps control changes to the individual components within each software version, while "configuration management" provides control over the complete version and the relationship of its components to one another. With configuration management all components of a given product or application can be organized, managed, and tracked as a unit.

The need for effective change and configuration management is now being felt in every type of business environment. Whether we are dealing with spreadsheets, documents, graphics, or ordinary text, we are all faced with the problem of controlling revisions and managing new versions that are being produced at such a rapid pace that manual controls cannot keep up. And the larger the project or application, the faster the problem can grow out of control.

Large banks have been particularly hard hit in trying to keep their computer systems up-to-date with all of the new products and services being offered to customers. For many, the mere thought of yet another overhaul to implement tax withholding on interest payments almost brought many bank computer systems to a halt. The problem is not so much in the software or computers themselves, but in the process of taping together new software routines to cover new operational needs. Without adequate documentation, for which there is never enough time, it is difficult to know the effect of a new software change on those made to accommodate product changes two years ago.

As the number of people who are involved with computers continues to increase, new procedures are required that can ensure the timely coordination and notification of these changes to all those whose work is affected. Again, manual efforts are of no avail. It is essential to have an automated solution like Softool's Change and Configuration Control (CCC) program, which is now commercially available for many different computers.

Evaluation

Softool's CCC is a software product that addresses the many special needs of computer managers and programmers, including audit requirements, and can benefit both scientific and commercial establishments. It has become a worldwide standard for automated change and configuration management and has been instrumental in establishing a new and much-needed product category within the software products industry.

> *I had one year after retirement when I did just what you would expect—travel, luncheons, needlepoint. But it was not enough for me. I felt I needed to be on a schedule for structure as well as stimulation.*
>
> —Evelyn Smith
> Un-retired Employee

THE TRAVELERS INSURANCE COMPANY

Un-retirement plan provides company with the valuable experience and mature judgment of trained and enthusiastic workers

The Program

In 1980 the Travelers Insurance Company conducted a pre-retirement survey of its 2,000 employees over age 55. Fully 85 percent of those who responded said they were interested in some form of employment following retirement and 53 percent said that their first choice would be to work part time for the Travelers. Only 12 percent of the respondents reported they had done "quite a bit" to prepare for their retirement, while 31 percent said that they had done no planning at all.

In light of these findings, the Travelers developed its "Older Americans Program." Its two objectives were to develop employment options for older workers and retirees and to help employees plan for their golden years.

The first step was to eliminate the mandatory retirement age that had been in effect throughout the company. The second step was to identify temporary employment opportunities within the company that could be filled by qualified retirees. Finally, positions that would lend themselves to job-sharing were targeted for those retirees who wanted to work only a few days each week. The Board of Directors supported these initiatives by increasing from 480 to 960 the number of hours an employee could work in a year without losing pension benefits. A Retiree Job Bank, co-administered by two job-sharing former retirees, was also set up at company headquarters in Hartford to match retirees with available positions.

In recent years, the Older Americans Program has been expanded to include both Travelers and non-Travelers retirees, and a recent job fair, called an "un-retirement party," collected job applications from 300 more senior citizens. Retirees are also being retrained (with pay) on computerized equipment in order to keep their skills consistent with business needs.

Evaluation

Today, 700 un-retired workers are listed in the Travelers Job Bank, helping to meet 60 percent of the company's temporary employment needs. The Travelers estimates that it saves at least $1 million a year by hiring its own retirees and relying less on more costly temporary employment agencies.

Those Travelers retirees who have returned to work say they are aware of the fact that the skills and experience they contribute make them a real asset to the company. Many of them also realize that expanded employment opportunities for older Americans increase our potential to improve both our productivity as a nation and our international competitiveness.

We seek to maximize our productivity at all levels through the proper use of capital, material, technology, and people. As part of our own principal strategies, we strive to promote effective two-way communication between employees at all levels and use new technology and management innovations to improve our operations.

—Ray Ybaben
Technology Manager

TRW INC.

Electronic mail system speeds decision-making process for diversified electronics manufacturer

The Program

At TRW, the traditional interoffice mail and telephone networks did not seem to be meeting the company's massive communication needs. So a number of corporate working committees were appointed to evaluate all the sophisticated computerized communications systems available on the market and to establish policies and guidelines for their possible use throughout the company.

When the idea of installing an electronic mail system was suggested, a task force was formed to identify and recommend appropriate vendors and to manage the pilot project. Though TRW manufactures computer-based systems itself, it had no prior experience in this area and decided that buying a system from an outside vendor would cost less than building one from scratch, even though the company had the technical resources to do so.

The system that the company finally decided on is fully programmable and easy to use. It allows all TRW employees to mail and accept messages from company offices nationwide. Each user has a private electronic mailbox where messages are received and stored, and has only to call up the system to have the mail personally delivered.

Receiving and sending messages, however, is only one advantage of TRW's electronic mail system. It also allows documents to be edited and transmitted without having to be completely retyped and monitors pending responses without senders and receivers having to contact one another to confirm receipt of a message. Some of the system's other features:

1. Messages can be forwarded by the receiver, along with any comments to a third party in order to answer an inquiry by the original sender.

2. Messages can be answered quickly and efficiently without both parties having to come together and without having to type formal replies.

3. Distribution lists can be standardized for any correspondence that needs to be sent to remote sales offices.

4. Any unit or department within the corporation can install its own computer bulletin board. A user has only to call up the board to find out if any new messages have been posted.

Evaluation

At TRW employees no longer have to synchronize telephone calls, worry about the differences between time zones, or engage in the frustrating game of telephone tag. Messages can now be checked during the regular workday, during off-hours, or while on travel, and that has helped cut the time lags between conversations and final decisions by 50 percent. The new electronic mail system has decreased company communications costs by 15 to 50 percent, depending on the distances involved, and increased overall communications productivity by an estimated 25 percent. Though its benefits have not been felt to the same degree among all TRW's operating units, it has succeeded in linking them far more effectively than traditional phone calls and memos ever could.

> *Considerable research experience suggests that the most successful adjustments occur when workers themselves decide which training or education they prefer or is most suitable to them and when they should participate in training or in mobility programs.*
>
> —Thomas J. Pasco
> Executive Director

UAW-FORD NATIONAL EDUCATION DEVELOPMENT AND TRAINING PROGRAM

Joint union/management training program benefits both auto manufacturer and its employees

The Program

Employee training and development was recognized as a major need in the employee involvement program developed jointly by the United Auto Workers (UAW) and the Ford Motor Company. To achieve this goal, the Employee Development and Training Program was established under the 1982 collective-bargaining agreement between the two parties and was expanded in the 1984 and 1987 agreements. The program is administered through the UAW-Ford National Education Development and Training Center in

Dearborn, Michigan, and is funded at the rate of 10 cents per worker-hour by the Ford Motor Company.

This innovative joint venture recognizes the important role continued training and development plays in increasing employee skills and quality of work life. It offers over seventeen different programs to Ford's active UAW employees as well as to those who are furloughed with recall rights. The four most important programs include Education Training and Assistance, National Vocational Retraining Assistance, Targeted Vocational Retraining, and Career Counseling and Guidance. The following is a summary of the program offered to Ford employees through 1989.

- Education fairs for 95,000 participating employees
- Life/Education Planning Program: provided opportunities for 32,000 employees to explore their personal strengths and interests and discover new ways to increase their personal growth through education and training
- Skills Enhancement Program: provided opportunities for 16,500 workers to continue their education, sharpen their skills in areas such as math or reading comprehension, and receive educational skills counseling
- Education and Training Assistance Plan (ETAP): provided 35,000 employees with prepaid tuition and compulsory fees (up to a maximum of $2,000 per year) for approved self-selected education
- Personal Development Assistance feature of ETAP: provided 13,300 employees with grants of up to $1,500 a year (within ETAP allotment) for personal development and training opportunities, including noncredit or nondegree courses
- College and University Options Program: included workshops to explore educational goals, in-plant college classes, and related support services
- Successful Retirement Planning Program: helped 9,000 workers and their spouses to plan their transition to retirement

- Career Day Conferences (employees involved: 8,900)
- Vocational Plans and Interest Surveys (9,100)
- Career Counseling and Guidance (10,000)
- Skills Enhancement (1,200)
- National Vocational Retraining Assistance Plan (4,800)
- Targeted Vocational Retraining Projects (1,500)
- Job Search Skills Training (4,200)
- Relocation Assistance Seminars (1,300)
- Relocation Assistance Loans (3,800)

Evaluation

A new and unique joint effort, the UAW-Ford Employee Development and Training Program is considered to be an important contributor to Ford's recent climb to the top-earning position among U.S. automobile manufacturers. And as a result of Ford's improved performance, some 152,000 Ford workers received $463 million in profit-sharing checks averaging $2,800 in 1989, based on the company's 1988 earnings.

> *Having rejected the traditional approaches,*
> *we faced a yawning void and a looming*
> *deadline. Of necessity we came to ask the*
> *single, simple question that provided the*
> *breakthrough: Why not measure input? In*
> *other words, why not quantify what it*
> *takes, in human terms, to do all the tasks*
> *our work requires—and then use that*
> *information to determine the most*
> *appropriate skill level for each task?*
> —Joseph N. Wolzansky, President
> Productivity Science Associates

WESTINGHOUSE ELECTRIC CORPORATION

Changing business realities spur nuclear
technology division to staff for service,
not design

The Program

The people at Westinghouse's Nuclear Technology Division (NTD) knew that their business was changing. The division was growing rapidly, but it was performing less power plant design and production work and winning more contracts for product application and service work. Did the division really need all the "superstar" engineers and scientists it was used to hiring? At first, no one really knew. So management decided to begin an investigation to determine whether the division's 3.5 to 1 ratio of engineers to technicians was still appropriate.

The goal was to develop a comprehensive, objective productivity plan that could project optimal staffing requirements for the future. The program that resulted was called Matching People and Work Requirements (MPWR) and since work output in the NTD was nonstandardized and sporadic, input measurements were used instead.

Staff members in the functional areas of design, analysis, testing, product assurance, nuclear safety, and computer methods development were consulted to determine all the discrete tasks that together defined the division's work. Employees were first surveyed to determine the time and importance of tasks they performed in the three areas of production, service, and R&D. Then five skill levels were matched according to the relative amount of time each would need to perform a given task. Twenty-three computer programs were developed to analyze the information, with accounting records providing control data.

Evaluation

The MPWR analysis revealed that the top-heavy work force was overqualified for much of the work that the division was now carrying out. In fact, employees had reported that 20–30 percent of their time was spent on activities that could be performed by less skilled personnel, even though these same employees felt that the work they were doing was important and necessary. Further analysis revealed that an enormous amount of time was being spent in training people on the job primarily due to seasonal mass hirings.

The NTD decided to change its personnel practices to spread hirings throughout the year and to bring more technician-level people into the division. Within a year, the engineer-to-technician ratio had fallen to 2.7 to 1, and an increase in employee satisfaction levels was also noted. "Payroll costs fell the predicted 8 percent in the first year," says Charles Hoop, division program manager. "When an organization systematically matches the skills of the white-collar employees to the work required, more people do what they're best equipped to do. And that's bound to increase productivity in human as well as financial terms."

Savings realized from the program have been averaging more than $1 million per year, and the MPWR has expanded to several other divisions and support areas within Westinghouse.

Application of MPWR outside Westinghouse has been equally successful. A post-LBO downsizing effort found $7 million in salary savings and $1.5 million in excessive costs. Employees embraced it because it was fair, not arbitrary. MPWR is available through computer networks and is in use in additional companies. End of 1989 results show savings wherever MPWR is used.

ACKNOWLEDGMENTS

We gratefully acknowledge the extraordinary efforts of those who have contributed to the quality and timeliness of the information provided in this book. Many managers provided direction for this project by telling us what they needed most in a handbook. Many readers from the workplace provided helpful and encouraging comments, and many successful companies were willing to share the formulas they found for gaining their competitive edge.

A very special thanks to Donna Mahon, Jacqueline Pace, Kevin Prins, James Reinsel and Nancy Skancke for their assistance in assembling and verifying information about companies and in editing and typing the manuscript; to Sally Seidman and Nancy Skancke for providing encouragement and perseverance; and to Jean Shepard and Fred Hills for their great help and guidance, always provided with good humor and patience.

INDEX

About the Authors

L. William Seidman has received national praise for his management of the savings and loan crisis. A graduate of Dartmouth College and Harvard Law School, he has been a successful businessman, a business school dean, and a distinguished public servant. He served as President Ford's economic adviser, and currently serves as Chairman of the Federal Deposit Insurance Corporation (FDIC) and the Resolution Trust Corporation.

Steven L. Skancke is vice president of G. William Miller & Co., a merchant banking firm. He directed the White House Conference on Productivity with Mr. Seidman during the Reagan administration. Both authors live in Washington, D.C.